DECEMBER'S Company

PAIGE HOCKMAN

December's Company by Paige Hockman

Published by Lee's Press and Publishing Company
www.LeesPress.net

Lee's PRESS — *A Premiere Self-Publishing Services Company*

All rights reserved 2024, Except for brief excerpts for review purposes, no part of this book may be reproduced or used in any form without written permission from Paige Smith.

This document is published by Lee's Press and Publishing Company located in the United States of America. It is protected by the United States Copyright. This book is a work of nonfiction. These are characters based on real people, they are not entirely a representation of those individuals.

Act, all applicable state laws, and international copyright laws. The information in this document is accurate to the best of the ability of Paige Smith at the time of writing. The content of this document is subject to change without notice.

ISBN-13: 978-1-964234-30-4
PAPERBACK

Table of Contents

Acknowledgements 1
Dedication 3
Prologue 4
Ch 1: The Beginning on Linsell Lane 5
Ch 2: T 10
Ch 3: Fresh Apples and Grief 24
Ch 4: Rose Finnley and Earl Rhoades 37
Ch 5: Who Ever Said You Need Permission to Borrow Someone's Bike? 49
Ch 6: July 28, 2007 54
Ch 7: Taking the Good with the Bad 59
Ch 8: The Fake Finnley and The First First Holy Communion 72
Ch 9: The Loneliest Days in 2010 82
Ch 10: The Aftermath 95
Ch 11: Simultaneously Weird and Wholesome 106
Ch 12: The MacHaughmans 120
Ch 13: Paper Mache, Gas, and a Triple Cheeseburger? . 133
Ch 14: The Moments We'll Remember 138
Ch 15: Blue Skies 150
Ch 16: Darkness. Then Light. 158
Ch 17: Reflection on Deep Loss 171
Ch 18: Amidst the Peonies 178
Afterward 182
About the Author 186

Acknowledgments

Mom and Dad, this one's for you. May the world learn to love you as much as I do.

Grammy, you are abundantly special. You kept your promise. I love you to the moon and back x10,000!

To my stepfather, E. Kids like me don't make it without people like you. You are one hell of a fisherman but an even better human being.

To my Godmother Sue and Uncle Semin, MacHockmans forever. Thank you for being willing.

R.E.F.—our friendship will now be preserved in time forever. I hope you inspire many to be true friends. They're desperately needed in this life.

B, thank you for always believing in me and loving me every day. It's an honor to be your wife.

Grandma Kay, thanks for all the love!

Meg & Patricia, thank you for loving and putting up with me all these years. XOXO.

To the real Finnley family—thank you, for it all.

Adam and Kelly, I have sometimes felt that the universe is never in my favor, but it must be to send me people like you.

To the ladies who stood by me on August 5, 2023, thanks for your continued love & support.

Mrs. Rettew, I hope this book helps to light the way for others like you always taught me to do. Mrs. Standley, for always believing (since 3rd grade) that writing was in my future. Mr. Frank, thank you for always believing in me. You saw past the brokenness; I am forever grateful. I hope I've made you proud. Dr. Malone, thanks for encouraging me when I was a teacher in training. Professor Hammond, your creativity still inspires me. Dr. Udelson, your support in my educational journey will never be overlooked or forgotten. To all of the amazing educators who have invested themselves in my future, without you I wouldn't be here doing this.

To everyone who has ever been there for me.

Dedication

To my sister, D, and brother, M. I have heard discourse surrounding if there is a perfect number. I believe it is three. May this book always be a tangible reminder of how much you are loved.

Prologue

The days of my childhood are abundantly special to me. And more than that, they are good. I think that is possibly a normal feeling when it comes to anyone's childhood, however, I feel it in my bones.

I have always known that I need to write this story. It will help so many people, and I cannot let my life simply come and go without introducing the world to beautiful people who were not given enough time. I did not invent these people, nor do I speak for them. I just wish to share my time knowing them so that others can know them too. I think they deserved more. In writing this, I also hope for some part of me to remain here once my days are up. I believe that is a legacy suited best for the writer.

This is my story of perseverance, and the people placed in my life so I could do so. To read it means you are entering into a place that is significantly meaningful to me and many others. I simply ask that you read it with care.

The names of things and people in this story were changed to keep dignity intact. Though my characters are based on real people, they are not entirely a representation of those individuals.

Thank you for taking the time to read my story. I hope you meet people you love while you're here, and I hope you leave here with an appreciation for the people around you and an understanding of the brevity of life. Life is merely a breath. And with that breath, I begin.

Chapter 1

The Beginning on Linsell Lane

I grew up on a quiet street called Linsell Lane in the small town of Cherish, Virginia. The fourth house on the left belonged to my great-grandparents on my father's side, who passed it down to my grandparents, who allowed my father to live there with his family after I was born. My dad spent time fixing it up, and we moved into the house when I was six months old. It was an old brick home with a front and back porch. In the front yard, a large tree off to the left side towered over the home alongside a gravel driveway to the right of the house. If you stood in the driveway and looked at the house straight on, you'd notice two small orange and yellow stained-glass windows built into the house, birthmarks of our quaint home.

The backyard held its own unique touches: a clothesline was nestled across the middle with a blue windmill attached. Behind the blue windmill was a blue swing set, which had begun to rust over but still worked just fine. The back porch overlooked a small garden where flowers and a variety of vegetables grew. A dark brown fence enclosed the backyard, and a few trees rested adjacent to it. The fence's exterior revealed the home's age. An additional tree sat outside the fence near the gate, and much like the tree in the front yard, it towered above the power lines and the backyard. Beyond our backyard fence and past the extraordinarily tall tree were acres upon acres that held a pond, woods, and abundant wildlife. Propped up against our fence was always Dad's rusted, old wheelbarrow.

My dad was an extremely talented carpenter, who owned his own business, which he called Haughman Home Improvements. He didn't believe he was talented to my understanding. An artist never appreciates their work. If they do, they run the risk of being vain. My dad genuinely discounted his work to himself and whether he realized it or not, to others. He didn't believe he was smart, and perhaps that was the first tragedy that made its appearance in my life. Though unseen, it was certainly real, and its remnants, unlucky.

Dad was from Virginia and had lived there his whole life. He was the ninth of twelve children, which made his growing up a special kind of beautiful and crazy. As I got older, he would tell me stories about having so many siblings, or I would hear stories from aunts and uncles. He was six feet tall with dirty blonde hair, blue eyes, and a smile that gave you hope. Everyone called him Timmy. My mother, Catalina, was stunning and hailed from Massachusetts. She moved down to Virginia a few years after her father was transferred to work in Washington, DC. She had two siblings, Uncle Dallas and Aunt Natalie, and was the oldest. She met my father on a blind date where she fell head over heels for all of Timmy's southern charm and blonde-haired beauty. She was about 5'5" and along with her Boston accent, she was blessed with a laugh that breathed life into you. People constantly commented on her contagious, remarkably distinctive laugh. When you paired her laugh with my dad's smile, the world was at its best. They made a gorgeous couple, and the old photographs don't do them justice, though they do make me wonder how they were never sought after to star in Hollywood films where they needed an insanely gorgeous couple, inside and out. My mom's 80s hair throughout the entirety of the 90s was iconic and unparalleled. All of that aside, I, Pia, am their first child. My Gram has told me about the day I was born. It was the afternoon on Christmas Eve. They got the news I had arrived, and Gram rushed to the hospital. Gramp had to work but made his way to the hospital as fast as he could. Gram ran into the parking lot to get him yelling, "It's a girl!!"

Gramp asked, "Is Catalina, okay? How did she do?"

Gram answered in tears, "She did great! She's great!"

I had made them grandparents. My mom had to be induced because I was supposed to be born two weeks earlier. I was comfortable and could've probably stayed in until January. Mom's doctor told her she "wasn't waiting until after Christmas, she was going to have this baby now," so that's how I ended up being born on Christmas Eve. It was meant to be. My parents couldn't smile at me harder in the pictures. They loved being parents to me and our life as a family of three, though I don't remember it, seemed as perfect as one could dream up. Two years and four months later, in April, my little sister, Delilah, was born. Two years and 11 months after that, my little brother, Timothy "Tim Jr" was born in late March. I don't remember anything about Delilah's birth, probably because I was only two. On the contrary, I remember almost everything about Tim's arrival into this world. Once Delilah and I got to the hospital, Dad took us down to the gift shop. He told us we could pick out a souvenir to remember the day our little brother was born. The hospital was a good size as was the gift shop. I turned the corner and saw Delilah staring at shelves of stuffed animal cats. There were so many stuffed cats; they had just about every color and pose. I reached up and grabbed the first one that caught my eye. She was a brown cat with white paws and a pink nose. She was perched in a standing position, and her whiskers looked so real. I was in my own world with my cat until I heard a crash. Delilah had climbed up the shelves of stuffed cats trying to reach the one she wanted. This caused several shelves to get knocked down. Cats covered the carpet of the gift shop floor. Dad came rushing over along with the ladies who worked in the gift shop. The workers displayed looks of anger and annoyance. Dad was flushed and embarrassed. He was also extremely apologetic. "I'm so sorry," he uttered. "I can pay for them all if you want," he continued. The ladies just picked them up and ignored Dad. Dad, standing in the mess of cats, asked Delilah which one she wanted. She pointed to an orange cat on the floor. Dad reached over one of the ladies, saying, "Oops, sorry." She glared at him, but he just smiled and took Delilah's cat to the counter to pay. When we got to the room with our stuffed cats, they had brought Tim back from getting bloodwork. Mom was holding him. Dad beamed and gently said, "Come here, girls. This is little Tim Jr. This is your little brother." The gift shop catastrophe was long forgotten, and I knew our family was complete.

Although we only knew a few of our neighbors, Linsell Lane had some peculiar and rather noteworthy residents. Mrs. Hazelton, Georgie Hazelton, was an elderly woman who lived next door. In the layout of houses on Linsell, hers was right before ours on the left side. She had the outline of a dark bird on the front of her house, and it had siding instead of brick, which was a rare occurrence on Linsell Lane. Inside her house smelled as if it hadn't been lived in for years. When you consider the fact that she never left it, that was impressive. My Mom told me once that Mrs. Hazelton had a fear of going outside. Due to that, she confined herself indoors most days. Dad took me to visit her once, and she introduced me to eggnog while I rode my scooter up and down her driveway. She was a kind woman, and that's what I remember most.

Directly across the street from our house lived Dewdrop and Elliston Franklin. Dewdrop referred to Elliston as "Eli", and she assured me numerous times that her name was Dewdrop. She reiterated that she had Native American ancestry. They were an older couple but not quite as old as Mrs. Hazelton. One house down from the Franklins lived Rob and Poppy, a middle-aged couple with two poodles. Poppy painted the poodles' nails pink on occasion, which made me giggle. The street ended in a cul-de-sac, where we would often venture on walks in our train wagon. The train wagon had 3 cars: a purple car for me, a green car for Delilah, and an orange car for little Tim. Unbeknownst to us, something sought us out until it could get close enough to crush us with a short, slight grasp. It preyed on beautiful things, and we had no power to stop it. It was one of those stories where you could see the end as it began. And somehow, before it came crashing down, you had already felt the impact of the fall.

Chapter 2

T.

Once his all-state wrestling days were far behind him, and he was all caught up on the carpentry, my dad could almost always be found in the yard. There was yard work to be done during every season and to prepare for each one coming up. He would cut trees down to make sure we had firewood to burn in the winter, cut the grass, weed whack, keep his garden up to date, trim trees and bushes, and so much more. He even built Grandma Haughman a pond in the backyard of her house using only his bare hands. I usually picture my dad with a pencil behind his ear because he was always putting something together or building something. Haughman Home Improvements often did well. Dad would get referrals, send estimates, and complete jobs; he was almost always given gifts from his customers and showered with appreciation. One evening in particular he came home with a 24 x 36 watercolor painting of a hummingbird, painted by the wife of a man he had completed a kitchen remodel for. Dad smiled ear to ear when he arrived home and immediately showed the painting to Mom, who gleamed in awe. It was a simple but darling painting that displayed four hummingbirds smelling two pink flowers. The dark background and the gold frame emphasized the birds and flowers. It must've taken the lady hours to complete it.

"Why did she give that to you, Dad?" I asked curiously.

Dad replied, "I asked her, and she said she knew when I started working that these would be the *best* countertops she had ever seen."

I stared at him in awe, for that was impressive to a little girl.

"What did you say, Dad?"

"I think I said something like, 'Aw shucks, Maryann. They were pretty old countertops!'"

Late one summer, we were hit by Hurricane Isla. We didn't live by the coast or anything, but our little town was affected quite intensely. I was only four or five at the time, but the tree in our front yard had grown a lot since first moving in and due to Isla, fell horizontally across the entire yard, thankfully somehow missing the house and vehicles. I was picked up from school early and watched as my dad and uncle worked tirelessly to get this giant tree out of our front yard. Dad and Uncle Dane both had chainsaws in hand and between the two of them were making progress fast. Still, so much of the trunk remained, and even though I looked out of the window, I could see the anguish in their eyes. Dad had put a bandana on, and Uncle Dane had taken off his layers. The chainsaw drowned out the rest of my thoughts that day.

I was the fifteenth grandchild on my father's side and the first on my mother's. Dad was used to people revealing a shocked expression when I mentioned how many siblings he had, so he would rarely say anything about the size of his family. He was proud despite keeping it on the down low. I always forgot the order of my aunts and uncles, so he would kindly remind me that it was Tabitha, John, Luna, Jemma, Meredith, Mitchell, Dolly, Geri, Dad, Dane, Kristin, and Shirley. I always messed the order up after Aunt Jemma but managed to get it back on track at Dad through the end of the list. Dad loved all his siblings but was the closest in age to Uncle Dane. They had a special bond. Aunt Geri recently recalled when Mom met them all for the first time. It was at a dinner party. She and Mom laughed, especially when Aunt Geri said, "I could see you were a little overwhelmed," to which Mom winked at her. She told Mom, Delilah, and me, "Your mother walked in with the perfectly teased 80s hair. She spoke, and I immediately clutched onto her Massachusetts accent. I nudged your Aunt Jemma and said, 'She's a Yankee!'" I laughed while Delilah took it in, and Mom acted like Aunt Geri's story wasn't real. Aunt Geri continued with, "I didn't think your dad was good enough for your mother!" As Mom lightly pushed Aunt Geri's shoulder in embarrassment, I just smiled. Mom was the most beautiful person I had ever seen, and the compliments were all understatements, even if she failed to acknowledge them in their entirety.

When I think of my dad, I think of quality time spent outdoors and soul-freeing laughter. I can't remember exactly when, but eventually, Dad got a black lab and named him Jack. Jack became a huge part of our adventures together. One of my favorite adventures to go on with Dad was wandering out into the massive field behind our house and looking for turkey feathers. While we were there, we would also let Jack run free without a leash since no one else was ever in sight. He would always retreat to us at the sound of Dad's whistle unless he saw a bird. Jack's favorite part of the field was the pond about a mile or two into the descent that he jumped into regularly. If it was wintertime and it happened to be frozen, he would glide across it joyfully.

One day, Delilah started joining us on our field journeys. Tim Jr. was still too young, but soon enough he was not too young for rides in the wagon down to the cul-de-sac on Linsell Lane. My memory is tattooed with an image of my dad in his white t-shirt pulling the train wagon with a huge smile on his face. As I glided down Linsell Lane in the wagon, I felt fearless. The sky fit so perfectly among the clouds, changing ever so slightly from day to night, and a glimmer of orange paraded in the sky as if it didn't want the part of the sky that was still blue to notice. I thought surely wherever we were in the world, it was the best place to be.

One day, Dad taught our cousin Kelsey how to ride a bike in our backyard. She was spending the night with us and hadn't ever ridden her bike without training wheels. She saw me ride and wanted so badly to not use her training wheels, but she was terrified. Dad comforted her, yet Kelsey was still so nervous. She was little but knew she wanted this! Dad helped her onto my bike and held her up while she pedaled. He explained to her what she would need to do. She kept saying in the smallest, tiniest voice, "I really don't think I can, Uncle Timmy," but he kept reassuring her, "Yes, you can, Kelsey. Just keep going. I've got you. I'm not letting go." He did this for about four to five minutes until he finally let go. Kelsey hadn't realized that Dad had let go, and she was riding her bike all by herself. When Aunt Jemma arrived to pick Kelsey up, she had a grin from ear to ear. Dad said it was no big deal.

Grandma and Grandpa Haughman owned three houses, technically four if you counted the one we lived in. They had a "regular" house, a mountain house, a lake house, and an inherited house. The lake house was less than an hour away, and Dad loved to take us there. I have so many memories of us swimming along with him. The house had a large dock out back with a table, chairs, and an area for their boats. There was also a crate of swimming noodles and life jackets. These were usually gone quickly because of how many cousins I had. Grandma and Grandpa Haughman had both a pontoon boat and a speedboat. There was also a small paddleboat they added later on. Right across from their house was a public beach area that we could swim to. When we were younger, we usually just got into the lake from the wooden ladder attached to the dock and enjoyed the water close by.

    One day at the lake house, I stood on the dock in my bathing suit. I was looking out into the water waiting until Mom or Dad got in so I could swim, too. I didn't have my life jacket on, and one of my aunts pushed me in. I guess to her it looked like I was debating on jumping or not, and she wanted to help me decide. I remember being under the water and desperately trying to swim up but not being able to no matter how hard I kicked my legs. Dad was right there and didn't even hesitate to jump in fully clothed to save me. When he got me back on the dock, I was shaken, and just remember hearing him say to his sister as he stood in soaking wet clothes, "Really? Why would you do that?" She responded that she didn't realize I hadn't learned how to swim yet. I don't know what would have happened had he not jumped in, but I certainly can't imagine it would have been good. The rest of my adventures at the lake house were much less terrifying.

    We spent every fourth of July at my grandparents' lake house for as long as I can remember. The neighborhood was a gated community, so someone either had to live there to get in or know someone who did. Grandma and Grandpa would have to call us in. "Haughman," Dad would say as we pulled up to the visitor entrance. They would usually ask for Dad's name, probably just out of the sheer amount of people in our family trying to get in under that last name. The community continued to put a lot of effort into their fireworks show each year. I have so many memories of being on the pontoon boat watching the fireworks sprint into the air. Fireworks on the lake were a lot prettier than watching them anywhere else. Since the Haughman family was so big, we would try to cram as many people on Grandma and Grandpa's pontoon as we possibly could, maneuvering people every which way. I remember the little jump I'd have to do to make it onto the boat. One day, the jump wasn't as big. Grandma and Grandpa would also take their speedboat out to watch fireworks to get the rest of the family on a boat. Whoever drove the speedboat would try to line up as close to the pontoon as possible when we got to where we wanted to anchor. Any leftover Haughmans or friends watched from the dock or screened-in porch.

On Christmas and Thanksgiving at Grandma and Grandpa Haughman's regular house, a line longer than the supermarket's would extend from the main table through half of the house. We would wait in such a long line due to the size of our family and the delicious meal that awaited us, sometimes saying things like, "I hope there's sweet potatoes left by the time I make it up there." We would then spread out through the whole home and yard to find a place to eat and chat. The holidays spent with my dad's side of the family were always the best. I will forever be grateful to have had such a big family to get together and spend time with. Not every child gets such a wonderful opportunity to be showered with love by so many aunts and uncles, so it will never be undermined. I miss those days so very much.

Other adventures with Dad would include jumping on the trampoline, jumping on him as soon as he opened the door from work, sitting by the fireplace in the living room in the winter, or begging him to buy you bunnies at the local rural retail store. A memory I have was Dad was picking me up from Uncle Dane's house one Saturday. I had been playing with my cousin Avery for a few days. Dad and Uncle Dane both worked in carpentry, had families to take care of, and had similar interests. So, it didn't surprise me when Dad got there that he stood in the yard and talked to Uncle Dane for what felt like an hour. Aunt Roxy told me that I could go outside and remind them that I was still there. It worked out for me to run outside when I did. Dad was talking to Uncle Dane about how he needed to go to the farm store in town. As I walked up, Uncle Dane asked Dad, "Ya know, if you're going to the one close to where you live, they're havin' their chicks and bunnies' sale now?" Dad looked at Uncle Dane with enlarged eyes as if to send him a signal to be quiet or stop talking. Dad then turned slowly over to me. The damage was already done. I had heard there were bunnies. So, I did what any young bunny-wanting girl would do. I begged. I begged with my heart and soul. If you didn't know this about my dad, he had a heart of gold and was a sucker for puppy eyes, especially when it came to his little girl. I didn't leave that store with one bunny. I left that store with two because Dad said it wouldn't be fair to get one for me and not also get one for Delilah. This moment taught me the importance of not forgetting others when you are getting something you really want, but it also gave me the brief delusion that life could be fair.

Dad was so into his yard work; he would often lose focus on what was around him. That was usually when my pranks took place. I remember one late morning when Dad was dressed up in khakis and a dress shirt. He wasn't wearing a tie, which admittedly, I thought was slacking a little. He was in the garden watering his plants when he set the hose down. I immediately took action! I hid in the bushes, grabbed the hose, and waited for him to come back my way. Once I heard the rustling of the grass, I jumped out holding the hose with a smirk on my face. He immediately put his hands up. Despite his plea not to do it, he already knew the idea was within me. I sprayed him down from head to toe, laughing mercilessly. I knew it was wrong, but it didn't make it any less funny. Besides, when he finally did get re-dressed, this time, he made sure to put on a tie. Dad was not one to hold grudges and that was who taught me not to hold them either. They didn't make sense. There were much more serious things that prowled about this life.

Dad called me Princess Pia and I knew he always had that in the back of his mind when he found himself doing the most ridiculous things for me. One morning, as my friend Marly was leaving our sleepover, her mom pointed out that there were bunnies loose in our backyard. They were outdoor bunnies that had dug underneath their cage and escaped. Our fence had slits in it, so if someone didn't stop them, they would never come back. I yelled, "DAAAAD!" When Dad got up, I told him what had happened quickly and anxiously as I shook with fear. He ran outside as fast as he could in his underwear to catch them. The bunnies were fast as lightning, and I hadn't thought that through. He was determined to catch them. Marly's mom chuckled slightly, and so did Zion, Marly's little brother. I wasn't laughing. I felt bad for Dad and was scared of losing our bunnies.

Not to mention it was kind of embarrassing that my friend and her family saw Dad in his undergarments. Marly, Zion, their mom, and I stood on the stoop by our side door watching Dad chase these bunnies around the backyard at barely eight in the morning on a Sunday. Mom was in the kitchen watching through the window. I did not have a good feeling, especially since it was so early, and the bunnies were so much faster than Dad. To my surprise, he caught Delilah's first and then mine and returned them to the cage. I was so grateful. Sadly, a few weeks later, they got out again. This time, in the middle of the night. We woke up to an empty cage and cried. Even though the bunnies got away, I will always remember Dad doing everything he could to catch and contain the two bunny rascals of Linsell Lane.

We got the news one evening that the owner of the field behind our home had sold it to a housing developer. Dad talked to Mom about what a shame it was over dinner but that "people need houses." We enjoyed the last few days and weeks we could get in the field before the construction truly began. The last time I ever remember Dad taking me on an adventure into the field, I glanced at Dad, who stared at the construction machines.

"Will you still take me back here even when it's a housing development?"

"Yes, of course," he assured.

I smiled and grabbed Dad's hand from the wheelbarrow.

"Maybe you'll make some new friends here, y'know. Once they build the houses."

I shrugged his comment off and tried to accept it. I wished we could keep the field forever. As I looked in the distance to the left, I could see a young girl about my age. She was brunette and as we got closer, she waved. I didn't know who she was, but it was awfully nice of her to wave to me. As I stared, Dad began to run again, pushing me forward in his wheelbarrow. I laughed crazily as Dad pushed me in zigzags all the way to the backyard. He yelled, "Trash! I have so much trash here. Where can I dump it?" The more he said, the louder I giggled. Maybe it wouldn't be so bad.

One thing Mom and Dad loved to do was take Tim Jr. out by the back fence so he could watch the bulldozers build the new houses. He giggled so much, but somehow, I was sure it brought Mom more joy than little Tim. This moment went from sweet to scary in an instant when Jack broke off his post and chased Delilah through the yard. She was able to get onto the trampoline and closed the liner, so he didn't get her, but he acted more aggressively lately. He had always been an overprotective dog and a loud barker. I can remember listening to him bark as I played in the yard alone thinking, *Will he ever stop?*

It was different now because Mom was concerned about our safety. The difference between Jack and other dogs was that other guard dogs usually recognized their owners and didn't act aggressively toward them if there was no threat in sight. Jack didn't let his guard down, ever. As much as I loved Jack, there was something off about him, and it wasn't worth the risk of a dangerous, tragic scenario. A few days later, Delilah and I were standing by the window in the living room staring out at Dad holding Jack on his leash in the backyard. He was taking Jack somewhere, and I just knew in my gut he wasn't coming back. I don't know if Delilah knew it, but I did. Mom didn't even have to say it. Dad walked inside and said, "Girls, wave goodbye to Jack. He is going to live on a farm down the road where he will have lots of room to run around and play. The owners of the farm are very excited to be getting Jack, and there are other dogs he will get to play with." Tears streamed down my cheeks, and all I wanted to do was retreat to my room. For as long as I could remember, Jack was there. I had been losing so much recently: the bunnies, the special field, and now Jack. Jack seemed indifferent through the window. I felt bad for him because I think he knew. I smiled and with the faintest bit of glimmer, showed him my last smile.

Dad called Delilah "Boo Boo" because she was always falling down, scraping her knees and elbows. It was odd if you saw Delilah without any scrapes, cuts, bruises, or band-aids on her. Dad would pick Delilah and me up and set us down one by one in his wheelbarrow. He would then push the wheelbarrow in a zigzag motion across the yard yelling, "Trash! Trash!" We would roar with laughter as Mom stood on the back porch with little Tim. Now and then, she would yell, "Be careful, Timmy!" as we laughed louder.

You should know that Timmy Haughman was a go-getter and a man with a plan. I remember one Christmas season we went to the local Christmas tree farm to pick out a tree for our living room. At this point, there was only one in the town of Cherish. I can't remember if Mom and my siblings were with us, but I don't think they were. I say that because I have this distinct memory of my dad saying to me, "I want you to pick out the tree, Pia." Perhaps that very moment was when my indecisiveness began. That was a daunting task for a six-year-old. I had no idea if I was going to be able to find a tree for our family. I knew it had to feel right, and it had to be the best one.

If you are wondering how I remember so much about my childhood and, in particular, my father, I am not sure either. It has been the mystery of my lifetime. I have always told people that it was because my body knew I would need to recall this information in great detail later on, so it saved space. I believe our bodies are amazing, and we don't give them enough credit for all they can do. My memory is a fascinating place. God may have known I would write this book and allowed me to access things in a way that others can't.

The Christmas tree farm wasn't crowded since it was only the first weekend of December. Dad had brought his ax to chop down whatever tree I chose. We walked through about two rows of trees before I saw one that caught my eye. I immediately looked at Dad and shouted, "THAT one!" He asked me if I was sure, and I grinned wholeheartedly. It was the perfect tree for our living room. It was tall but not too tall, plump but even, and it didn't look beat up. I was so excited.

It was almost comical that as soon as Dad chopped that tree down and threw it over his shoulder, a man came out of nowhere and hissed at Dad. He cried, "You know, sir, you're not really supposed to chop down the tree yourself. We have people here to do it for you."

Dad replied genuinely, "Oh, my bad. I had no idea," and continued to carry the tree to the counter to pay.

The man continued to harass Dad, and demanded, "Please let me carry that for you."

Dad glanced back and immediately forward again and said nothing.

"SIR. I am going to have to ask you to put the tree down." Dad kept walking. The man continued, "PUT THE TREE DOWN, SIR."

Dad finally turned around, so sure of himself, and said to this man calmly, "Hey, I've got it" and resumed walking. We paid and took the tree home. I guess they had to do that because people sometimes stole trees. Although, I'm still not sure what difference it would have made if they had cut the tree down for us. They could see the tree way up on Dad's shoulder. He was six feet tall; we clearly weren't planning on stealing it.

I giggle sometimes when I think about my dad walking into that tree farm with his ax, chopping down his own tree, throwing it over his shoulder, and then getting harassed by a small man because he didn't get to chop it down or carry it for us. I'm not sure why my brain chose to remember that experience, but it is likely for a reason. I think it taught me that as we prepare for December's company and all things Christmas, we need to involve our children in those experiences because that's what the holidays are truly about. It also taught me that going after what you want in life doesn't come without interruptions and hardship. People may sometimes try to make you feel like you are in the wrong. They may even come at you or cause a scene. When you know what you are doing and why you are doing it, keep calm, keep walking, and carry your tree high. Our illegally cut tree looked another level of lovely that year.

Dad was used to throwing the old Christmas trees into the field behind our house where they would either rot or decompose. Since they had started clearing it for a future housing development, he had to take the tree to the dump. At least it was another adventure to go on. After the dump, Dad needed to fill up on gas. We pulled over at one of the main stations in town about a mile from our house and stopped at gas pump number three. I stayed in the car as Dad pumped gas. An older man who looked a tad scruffy came up to him and started talking. I couldn't hear what they were saying, but Dad opened the door and reached in to grab his wallet. He handed this man a $20 bill and waved him a good day. I vocalized my concern once Dad got back in the car.

"Dad, what did that man want?"

"He wanted money, Pia. He said he couldn't afford his gas."

"Oh… you gave it to him?"

"I did. I can't always, but I had a few extra dollars on me this time." I was amazed at the kindness Dad showed. He didn't know the man he just helped. He could've been lying, but Dad saw the good in everyone.

Chapter 3

Fresh Apples and Grief

I don't remember when it all changed, but somewhere it did. Dad's carpentry business had started to decline, and our family struggled financially. When Mom asked me to get ready to go out to eat with Dad, I did as she asked. He was going to meet us at a buffet in the town square. As we sat down, we waited a few minutes for him to get there.

When I saw him walk through the door, I yelled, "Mom, there's Dad!"

Dad was dressed in a white polo shirt with khaki pants; he looked put together and handsome. The waitress took our drink orders. I ordered chocolate milk, and she brought all our drinks quickly. I grabbed a straw. I also noticed there were some coloring sheets on the table, so of course, Delilah and I helped ourselves to those. Mom and Dad were talking, but I zoned out as I colored. My blue crayon had rolled away, and when I tried to grab it, I knocked my chocolate milk all over the table. It soaked the menus and my coloring sheet and even got on Dad. It was on the floor now and starting to leak onto the booth we sat in.

Dad started yelling at me. I had never heard him yell like that before. He was being loud and with seemingly no awareness of just how loud he was. I started to cry, to which Mom told him, "Look what you made her do, Timmy. Just sit down."

I let Dad know that it was an accident, but he continued

to speak with angst about what a mess I had made.

In my sadness, I said in my bravest voice, "You're the worst!"

Dad walked out of the restaurant while I continued to cry a river of tears. I didn't mean he was the worst; I just didn't understand why he made such a big deal out of it. People were looking at us, but I didn't care.

That was the day I learned that some moments live with us forever, not because they are good, but because nothing better succeeded them to negate their poor quality. They live in us forever because they remain as the last. And you always want the last time to be good if it's truly the last. I didn't know it then, but that was the end of my innocence and our family as I knew it.

On May 27th it was sunny, and I thought to myself *how nice of a day it was. Everything was so peaceful. The teacher was reading my favorite book to the class.* All of a sudden, the phone rang. "Pia," said Mrs. Reese, "you're leaving."

I was thoroughly confused. If I was ever getting picked up early from school, I was always made aware by Mom. I felt deep confusion in my gut. I knew something was wrong. Gram waited inside the door of the office for me. It took a while for me to get there since I had to carry everything from my classroom to the other end of the school. I opened the door and Gram simply gave me a soft smile. All she managed to utter was, "Let's go."

I walked with her out to the car, and she drove away from my school without saying a word. The most real moment of my life came at such a young age. I desperately wanted an answer, but I also wanted to go as long as possible without knowing. What a contradiction. "Mrs. Reese was reading my favorite book…" I said, hoping it would spark something, hoping I was wrong. Gram just smiled again at me, as if her eyes were pitying the very seat I sat in. She drove all the way to her house, which was an hour away. I got out of her car and immediately ran out back to play on her swing set. If she wasn't going to speak to me, I was going to make the most of the rest of my day. After all, I didn't even get to listen to my favorite book all the way through.

Once a few hours had gone by, I noticed Aunt Natalie had arrived and was hugging Mom. They were both crying. The same gut instinct I had in the car after Gram picked me up from school had unfortunately returned. Something wasn't right. I knew eventually someone would tell me. Delilah and Tim Jr. played inside and right as I looked through the sliding glass door, Mom opened it and said, "Pia, I need you to come inside," wiping tears from her face. This was the moment I was hoping we could put off forever. Holding Tim, Mom said, "Girls, I need you to sit down." We complied, looking at each other and then towards Mom. "Girls," Mom sniffled. "Your Dad died today." I immediately stormed off to lock myself in the bathroom. I was far too young to truly understand the gravity of what Mom had just said, but somehow, I knew it was bad.

It happened so quickly. He was here, and then he was gone. Snatched from our lives too soon. There was absolutely nothing we could do to change it.

Beautiful people were too often temporary. My childhood was the fleeting breath of life that was summer. Its warm vitality pulled me in effortlessly. As it sat in front of me, I believed

I had adequate time to enjoy it, and before I knew it, the leaves were beginning to turn. It ceased before I wished it would, and it took its toll on me to recover, sometimes feeling like a process I would never heal from. When we were in its embrace, I had never seen anything so beautiful. And that changed me for the rest of my life. It implanted in me hope that was undying. Whether I knew it or not, my life was beautiful, and the trace of its hand no matter how rough did not leave me bitter, but rather forever changed.

The front door opened every hour the following week with people bringing us cards, meals, and anything they thought would be useful. It was mostly people from our small church and parents who knew us because their children attended school with either me or Delilah. The one thing a lot of people dropped off was apples. I had never *seen* so many apples. I didn't even know this many apples existed. There was a whole basket of them up to my knees by the wall in the living room. Not that I was extraordinarily tall, but that's a lot of freakin' apples. As I looked at the apples, I felt pissed. I never knew fruit could make you angry…grief was strange.

I found Mom in the kitchen with Gram and blurted out, "What do people think we are going to do with so many apples?"

"They are just trying to be nice, Pia," Mom gently responded.

"I think someone at the church lives on an orchard, or near one," Gram added.

"Oh," I managed to respond back.

I'm not sure I understood it yet. The ways our lives had changed forever. The many ways I would change. There were signs, and it started with the new manner in which people looked at me. The way they looked at me said it all without them even speaking a word. They didn't envy me. They felt sorry for me, Delilah, and Tim Jr. Most people seemed to feel bad for Mom. We didn't live in a city, and people talked. The grocery store was where I felt it the most. There and school. I was getting tired of the looks that whispered *I don't know how they will make it, but we'll pray they'll be okay*, or *Bless their hearts. So young, too.* I think that's when I decided I didn't want people to feel sorry for me. Just because Dad was so young and all of us were young didn't mean we weren't going to make it. I didn't see Mom cry, but I knew she did. She had to. She was adjusting to being a single mother to three young children. I just hoped I didn't add stress to her life. As the oldest, my new role was to step up, be good, and carry on quietly.

 I think the first time it actually hit me was in December of '04, about seven months after Dad's death. I had gotten out of Mom's minivan. It was dark out. Cold. Mom was gone taking Delilah and Tim Jr. inside after they had fallen asleep in the car. I felt the faintest bit of melancholy as I realized our house was the only one on our street without Christmas lights for as far as I could see. It made sense since Dad would've been the one to do that. I became acquainted with the fact that we were missing something. We were also literally in the dark. It probably took me seven months for it to truly sink in due to my ripe age of seven years paired with the fact that Mom was truly amazing, the most dedicated mother to her three children. As I've gotten older and reflected on those early years, I've been in total awe of her strength. She lost the love of her life and amid her own grief, she still woke up each day and gave us the best life she could. What a blessing and what a woman.

It wasn't until roughly four years after his passing that I found out the truth behind my father's death. We were in the car when Delilah abruptly asked Mom, "How did Dad die?" I remember immediately wondering to myself how I had never bothered to ask her that same question…seriously. Mom inhaled the deepest of breaths and said in reply, "I was waiting to tell you until you asked, or you were old enough for me to bring it up. I guess it's okay for you to know now." Mom's hands gripped the steering wheel as she looked out at the road. Mom continued, "Your dad struggled with addiction… and… he… overdosed."

There was a long pause. Confusion was the first emotion I remember feeling. *How had I just now found this out? I had no idea. Blindsided.* I was doing so well on my journey through unexpected grief, and now I basically had to start all over again. This was a whole new thing to process, totally different than what I was doing. Over the years, I have dealt with and still do deal with certain emotions: frustration, disappointment, and, most of all, plain sadness. I used to be filled with shame. It was all-encompassing, and I certainly didn't want people to know the truth behind how my dad died. I even lied to one person and told them it was an accident. To make me feel better when I admitted this, Mom said it *was* an accident, that he *wasn't trying* to die how he did, but still, I knew I omitted some truth. I didn't *owe* anyone the truth, but I didn't want to share it willingly. Since then, I have healed in a variety of ways, so much so that now I am writing a book about it. It truly is a process. Grief is the longest process, one that spans a person's entire life. It never truly ends. Grief isn't linear either.

I so often forget this. It usually comes when I am angry at myself for having a moment of difficulty, feeling as if I'm not where I should be, or I've already been in the spot I'm struggling with.

I don't feel qualified to speak on addiction, even still. I have learned there are many various types, but more than that, there are many people who struggle or have struggled with addiction. I am only sharing my small perspective of how my father's death affected mostly me, but also my family. Even though my siblings and I went through the loss of our father at the same time, if either of them was writing this book, I have no doubt it would be different. Even though we all lived it, it was not the same for each of us. Many different factors made the experience its own for each one of us. For me, I am the oldest, so I remember the most. I also had to mature quickly, help Mom, and take on a secondhand motherly role.

This leads me to an analogy I thought of. If we think of ourselves as puzzles, we are all made of different pieces and numbers of pieces. Sure, we all go on to create a beautiful picture when pieced together through time, and deep down we are all puzzles, but my unique pieces are ultimately what create my individual picture. Every puzzle is not supposed to turn out the same. This is a lot like life, too. We are all living our own lives, and the perspectives we have are created by the experiences we endure along with how we handle those experiences. The hardest thing has been to not become offended by someone else's view of my father's death. While some may sugarcoat it, it comes with a lot of hurt for me. I was a child. I have to remember that others are a different puzzle with many pieces distinct to only them. They are not necessarily supposed to understand how his oldest daughter felt, and I am not supposed to understand how his death affected them. Perhaps my words can lend some perspective into the depths of my heart. That's all we can do to help others understand; write what we know. I write this with the utmost care.

To tell you the truth, my heart breaks for my father. He was so loved and such a beautiful soul. He should have done and seen so much more. I also think grief is different when you are a child, dependent upon a person for survival. My life has been significantly harder because of this terrible situation. My siblings' lives have been more difficult, too. At one point, I resented my father for that. You are no longer living for just yourself when you have children. I have hated watching my siblings suffer because of my father's addiction and overdose. It has hurt my family too, immediate and extended. The dynamic will never truly be the same. On the other hand, the truth is that once your loved one becomes addicted to a harmful substance, they are no longer thinking or acting as the same loved one that you knew before. This has made it easier for me to understand when questions come to mind such as: *how could my dad have done this to his three young kids?* Well, that wasn't my dad acting as the man I knew and loved. That was my dad thinking and acting like someone struggling with addiction, a stranger to the Dad I've described. My Dad will forever be Chapter 2.

In our society today, we are often made to think things have to be one or the other, that they cannot possibly be both. Two things can be true at once. You can speak about addiction's effect on your life, but that does not mean you are speaking negatively about the person struggling with addiction. You can be a good person and struggle with addiction. You can be disappointed in someone's actions and still love them so much. It would be a lie if I wrote this book shrugging off the effect of addiction on my life.

To add to that, while addiction is a disease, and genetics do play a factor, I have always felt accountability is a form of love. I also think it's important to work to eliminate the shame and stigma tied to addiction. No one should be embarrassed to talk about their struggles or the struggles of a family member. Talking openly about struggles will help other families who will find themselves in a similar place in the future. It also helps those families and individuals struggling now. The more people talk about addiction, the easier it will become for people to talk about addiction's harmfulness. It's powerful to share the struggles you have endured with others.

For a long time, I was scared to share my story. I worried a lot about so many different things. I know this is something I have to do, and I view it as my father helping other people long after his death. I do believe, if my father had survived, he would want people to know everything. He would want people to know how much your kids and family will suffer. He would want people to know the reality of how harmful addiction's grasp is. He would want those who struggle to know how valuable their life is, and how much is waiting for them on the other side of life.

I also want to mention how casually addiction can creep into your life. For my father, it wasn't this momentous moment followed by years of struggle. It was a single, relatively normal moment and day. He met someone at work, and it drowned his old life away. He didn't struggle for very long before he was gone. He wasn't someone you would have looked at and thought struggled. It can be the person you least expect, the person you think has it all together, the person with a family, the person good at their job.

Research from the American Addiction Centers and The National Institute of Health provide powerful insight into the lifelong effects of addiction on children. In a Guide for Children, American Addiction Centers wrote, "In homes where one or more adults abuse alcohol or drugs, children are approximately twice as likely to develop addictive disorders themselves, according to Current Drug Abuse Reviews. These children are also more likely to experience poor performance in school, emotional and behavioral problems, low self-esteem, a higher risk of physical, verbal, or sexual abuse, a higher risk of developing anxiety or depression, earlier onset of experimentation with drugs or alcohol, and a greater chance of becoming addicted once they start using drugs or alcohol," (Editorial Staff, February 2024).

I suffer from anxiety and depression now. My mental health ebbs and flows. I do not label that solely as a result of early exposure to addiction but rather as the result of many external things in my life that have impacted me internally. Addiction is one thing that has left a lasting effect on my life. It will never go away. People have said that my father was a risk-taker and may have had an addictive personality. Some people do not understand, but even though I don't consider myself a risk taker (we'll overlook the fact that I took a huge risk by putting my life story in the hands of the world) or share that personality type, I still know I've been exposed and need to be careful. I try to be diligent about not drinking often. When I choose to drink, I have only one. In addition, I decide on a few months throughout the year where I don't drink at all, and I don't allow myself to have any alcohol in my home during these times. This helps keep me aware. Even though I don't necessarily worry about myself, the awareness of how easily addiction can happen is key to being an advocate for yourself. I encourage everyone to pay more attention to their health and the health of their family.

Addiction is a very real thing. I am no expert on it. I have never struggled myself. I have known friends who have struggled, family members who have struggled, and have read the stories of strangers who have shared their addiction struggles with the world. No one who suffers is alone. The craziest part is that I never *fully* knew my dad was struggling. Once I found out, I pieced one incident together that my dad attempted to shield me from. I can appreciate the sentiment of him trying to protect me, and it just goes to show that despite it all, he was a good dad at heart. I already knew that, by the way. I have no way of knowing what other things I would have had to overcome had he not attempted to protect me from his addiction; still, a parent cannot entirely shelter their child from the evil that has crept into their home. Children know more than you think they do, and they are incredibly intuitive. Eventually, they find out the full truth, if not from you, from someone else. It is best to accept that your children will always find out everything. Though I was young, in my earlier grief, I wished I had known the whole truth back then. I thought that I would've gotten to this place of peace in my life faster, but it was probably for the best that I didn't know then.

Regardless, nothing could have prepared me to find out, and no one could have changed what had already happened. On an early June day in 2004 at only seven years old, I stood up and read a prayer at my father's funeral. I don't think there was a dry eye in the room.

Many years later, I majored in English in college. My university had the most wonderful English department. Each professor stood out in their own special way. I will never forget my professor in my African American Literature class and a point she made one day. I cannot recall exactly what it was we were reading at the time, but we were discussing slavery. She gently educated a student after he had spoken. She told him that these people did not choose to be slaves so calling them slaves makes that their identity. If we refer to them as 'enslaved people' rather than as slaves, it reminds us that they were humans being abused against their will. Slavery was not their identity. This taught me that people are not what holds them captive. We are not what we struggle with, and our identity does not rest in the terrible experiences we endure, no matter what those may be.

I should mention that I am by no means comparing my father to an enslaved person. I just learned a lot from my professor's point at this moment in the course, and I think it is an incredibly powerful point that can apply to so many situations. I am not sure why it is so easy for us to label ourselves with what burdens us, but we are so much more than our pain. We need to work harder to change the diction we use when speaking about ourselves and our struggles. Your identity is not your depression, your anxiety, your addiction, your fears, your illness, or your mistakes. The way we speak has more of an impact than we think it does. Remind yourself of that today. You are not what holds you captive, so let that set you free.

    As for my dad, his identity was not a drug addict. He was someone who had bad influences in his work life and struggled with addiction for a brief period. He was and always will be so much more than that. He was loving and genuine, skilled, passionate, and athletic. He was kind. He was a husband, father, son, sibling, uncle, and friend to many. As for me, I choose to focus on the sunny days. You are present. We are riding down the street in our train wagon. You are there. Alive. Happy. You are just out in the garden in your white tank top planting in the sweltering sun. You are out back fetching the wheelbarrow. I can see you from the window. I am waiting for you where it all began.

Chapter 4

Rose Finnley and Earl Rhoades

I walked into the kitchen as Mom peered out the little window on the door of the back porch. After Mom saw me enter the kitchen, she glanced at me for a moment until I said, "What?"

"Come here for a second," she said, as she continued looking out the window.

"Yes?" I asked, hoping to be impressed.

"The construction looks to be done at this end of the neighborhood, and look what they built right outside our back fence?"

"Wha—" I stopped mid-word. "A cul-de-sac." She just smiled.

Cul-de-sacs would always remind me of Dad. I guess it's good that this one was a lot closer, and Mom could keep an eye on me better. I had recently been given a new bike and I thought to myself that the new cul-de-sac would be the perfect place to ride it.

Just minutes later, I told Mom that I was going to take my bike out to the new neighborhood and ride. She was fine with it, as long as I didn't venture too far from our house. I pushed my bike through the yard, opened the rickety old latch attached to our back gate, and once my tires hit the pavement, I hopped on. As I rode around, I observed all the new houses. Surprisingly, they did not all look the same. There were not a ton of different layouts, but two specifically that I noticed. There were four houses directly in the cul-de-sac and a fifth that was sort of halfway in it. Six if you count ours that was just slightly behind it but still really close. Families were moving in, and some already had. I rode down the street connected to the cul-de-sac all the way to the stop sign and back up. As I made my fifth or sixth lap around the new circle, I wondered how long the cul-de-sac had been finished and I just never noticed. The last year or close to one had truly flown by without Dad, and I guess I had spent less time outside without him around, probing me for adventure.

A young girl about my age was running up the street toward me on my bike. I was a little introverted, so I started to panic. What did she want? Once she reached me, she immediately said, "Hi. I'm Rose. How are you?"

I was a little tired from riding my bike but managed an, "I'm good. How are you?"

She smiled as she asked, "Are you going to tell me your name, or is it a secret?"

"It's Pia. My bad. Um, I live over… *there*," I said pointing to the old brick house behind us.

Quickly, she said, "That's cool, I live there," pointing to the third house on the street connected to the cul-de-sac. I squinted and could see it read "Daisy Court."

"That's funny," I said under my breath.

"What is funny?" Rose questioned with her hands on her hips.

"That your name is Rose, and you live on Daisy Court."

She gave me a half-smirk; her hands were still on her hips.

I continued, "My bike also has daisies on it. I got it for Christmas a few months ago!" I had the sudden realization that I was on my bike and Rose was just standing there. I felt bad, so I told her, "We could go swing if you want, on my swing set. That way we both would have something to do." Rose nodded cheerily. "Do you want to come meet my mom first? She's inside, but I'm sure I can get her to step out on the porch."

"Yeah, that's fine!" Rose assured me.

"My dad died a few months ago, or I'd have you meet him too. I used to come out here with him before there were any houses built. You would've loved him."

Rose answered, "I know. I saw you with him a few times. He seemed like a good dad," which threw me off. And she went on to say she saw me in his wheelbarrow, and she was sorry that he died. I kept thinking of what she meant by that she had seen me before. *How was that possible?* I wondered as we inched closer to my house.

I pounded on the back door trying to get my mom to open it. I didn't want to disappoint my new friend. Mom answered the door wide-eyed holding Tim, likely expecting an explanation as to why I was incessantly banging on the door.

"Do you want to meet my new friend?" I asked hopefully.

"I can, but it'll have to be quick, Pia. Your Grandpa just got here to fix the plumbing issue, and I'm cleaning up a few things. Gram will be here soon too, to watch you guys while I prepare for my interview tomorrow.

My Mom waved to Rose from the back porch. Rose waved from the swing. I gestured her over.

"Hi, miss. I'm Rose. I live in the new neighborhood."

"Hi, sweetie. I am Pia's mom. That's awesome that you are both around the same age and can play together. Do you girls want some ice pops?" I looked over at Rose who had a twinkle in her eye and told Mom that I would go get the box of them. When I came back outside, another little girl was walking up to our fence, along with a little boy. She was much younger than us and he appeared younger too, but older than the girl. After Rose grabbed an ice pop, she noticed my confused expression, turned, and said those were her siblings, Rayne and Jedediah. We hadn't completely closed the fence, and they made their way in too. I offered them ice pops as well. They both took one.

Rayne was so small and had cookie crumbs all over the lower half of her face. She seemed to follow Rose around everywhere. Shortly after we finished our ice pops, Jedediah told Rose that their mom wanted them home soon. As they were leaving, it hit me. I realized where Rose had seen me before. She was the little girl waving at me from the end of their plot, which was now their driveway one of the last times Dad and I were out in the field. "Hey! I reali…" but as I spoke, they were already out of earshot. The long grass by our old fence swayed with the wind as I watched them recede into the distance.

A few weeks later, I met Rose's family, the Finnleys. The Finnley's house was yellow with maroon shutters. It had the steepest driveway in the whole neighborhood. I found out later they had the steepest driveway in the entire town of

Cherish. Rose was one of six children. Considering that I was from half of that, I was amazed. I told her about my dad being one of twelve and thought about how her family was half of that. There was Mr. Finnley, Mrs. Finnley, Rose's older brother Joshua, who went by Josh, and her five younger siblings: Jedediah, who sometimes went by "Jed"; James, who was called Jimmy, Rayne, and Jamison, who most of the family referred to as Jamie. Jamie was little.

They were a Christian family from the many crucifixes I could see, and their house was full of so much commotion and love. I felt like my house was too quiet, especially these days.

Being at the Finnleys made me happy. It seemed like there was always someone to play with. They were trying out their new snow cone maker and several of the other neighborhood kids were over too. It was probably because of the snow cones. Rose told me that I could have a snow cone, but I'd have to wait in line. Who wouldn't want to wait for a snow cone? I could see the many flavors of syrup Josh had set out, and I eyed the pink one.

Before I returned home, I walked straight to Dewdrop's house. Eli had fallen off a ladder a few days ago and hurt his neck. I checked in to see if I could do anything, but Dewdrop reassured me, "Probably not. But thank you." My favorite thing to do at Dewdrop's house was to pick up pinecones in her front yard and then go in for some milk and cookies. She always had pinecones in her yard, and she rarely let me leave without offering me cookies. She had a basket of pinecones on her coffee table too. I almost always added one or two to it before I left. I'm not sure if she ever noticed. Once Dewdrop got a minute, she asked, "Doing okay, sweetie?"

"I'm doing the best I can, ma'am. Thank you for asking." She just smiled.

To my surprise, in my kitchen was a random man who I had *never* seen before. He was fixing our refrigerator, and I just knew it was not someone Mom had hired. I didn't even know our fridge was broken. I stopped dead in my tracks when I saw him. He was on his knees and looked up saying, "Oh, hello." I had no interest in conversing with him.

I found out a few months later that the random man in my kitchen was a man by the name of Earl Rhoades. Mom had started a new job a little while ago, as a receptionist at a commercial water testing company, and it turned out that Earl had beaten another guy to ask Mom out. Mom wasn't quite sure about dating, and the first time Earl asked, Mom told him exactly that. Earl indicated that he understood but asked Mom just to think about it. He came back around a week later and asked Mom again if she had gotten a chance to consider his request. Mom still wasn't sure and let Earl know that she had three young kids who had just lost their dad two and a half years ago, so it was probably best if she passed up the offer. Earl listened and let Mom know that he would really like to take her out on just *one* date. Mom waited a second and declared she would go. Earl understood it to be the "best first date there ever was."

I wasn't too sure about Earl at first, and I'm pretty sure he knew my thoughts about him. As for Delilah and Tim Jr, they formed an alliance with him simply because he was someone to sneakily jump on when he opened the door. They found a lot of fun in that. I thought about how I used to do that with our dad, which felt like forever ago. Delilah and Tim Jr. spent a lot of time together. They were pretty much the same height despite their three-year age difference. Either Delilah was a little small or Tim Jr. was growing like a weed. It was probably a little of both. I often felt disconnected from the two of them. Something happened to me as the oldest child after the loss of a parent so young.

When I realized Earl wasn't going anywhere, and after I vented my third-grade teacher's ear off, I figured I had to drop my attitude. I still didn't like that it felt like he was taking the place of my dad, but I knew it wasn't his intention to do so. He sensed the attitude and tried to reassure me of that once. That same day, Earl was sitting out back alone, so I asked him, "How old are you?" because I couldn't tell. He looked older than Mom but not a lot older. He asked me how old I thought he was. I took a second, looked at him intensely, and responded that my guess was forty-five. I remember it so clearly. He said, "I'm *not* forty-five, Pia," turning his head ever so slightly to the side. I asked him the question again. He said he was fifty-eight. I was thrown for a loop on that one. He certainly didn't look fifty-eight. Mom was thirty-eight. I just said, "Oh. You don't look it."

Earl was pretty darn interesting, come to find out. He had two children of his own who were much older than my siblings and me. There was Jessica, who went by Jessie, and Tiffany. Jessie lived way out in Colorado. I asked him one afternoon why she lived out there, and he said it was because she went out that way one time to visit some friends. She came back, and all she could talk about was how much she loved it out there. He just knew she was going to call Colorado home, and one day, she did.

Whenever I spoke about school, Earl would tell me, "I never was the best student, Pia." It was as if he was trying to let me know that I could talk and he would listen, but I shouldn't expect a lot of engagement or any advice on the school thing from him. I also probably shouldn't ask for his help on any homework assignments. He went to a Catholic military school in Washington, DC. "A true Catholic military school," was how he described it. He went there with his older brother, Benny. He told me it was extremely strict, as military schools usually are. I'm not sure what happened there, but he was turned away from church. He loved the Lord in his own way, and often told me that, but didn't feel the need to attend a service every Sunday. From the way he talked about it, I knew it was because of his military school days, even if he neglected to tell me exactly why. He did mention that the nuns had rulers, and I put the rest together.

He went to art school when he was 19, but he dropped out a year later. He lived in California for the "better part of ten years," where he trained and broke thoroughbred racehorses. Earl made sure to specify that while he did break a few horses, he was not a true rodeo man. I asked him how he ended up in California and he said he followed a girlfriend out there. "Young love," he said, "it's powerful." His brother, Benny, lived in Louisiana, and he had visited New Orleans for Mardi Gras with Benny for seven straight years. I heard some stories about those days.

He was in a band for a while called 'Rhoadin' and Rollin.' They played locally at different bars and restaurants. After the band parted ways, he DJed for a while with his band equipment and some new gear. He would still occasionally pick up a job here and there, but it wasn't his full-time gig by any means. He worked with horses here in Virginia too. He did the same tasks as when he was out in California, but what was cool was that here he worked with the 1981 Kentucky Derby-winning horse while he was at Bernard Farm. The horse's name was Shadow Racer. He had also worked as an exterminator and crawled under houses to give details about what needed to be done and how much it would cost each customer for the job. He described it as a "tough way to make a living." He also drove a commercial truck for a nursery and farm. Now, he worked with Mom and had been at the company for over twenty-three years. He was the company's warehouse manager. The warehouse was a two-man mission, just Lloyd and Earl every day. They rarely rested. To add to Earl's hats, he was an avid fisherman. He told me fishing was not resting, not the kind of fishing he did. He grew up fishing on the Chesapeake as a kid and now had his own boat and went fishing just about every weekend from the opening weekend in May to the last day of the season, December 31st. Mom was the first mate. I was the lowest rank, unfortunately. He said I had to work my way up.

It turned out that Mom and Earl really were twenty years apart. I never thought about what other people would think but found out when I got older that a lot of people didn't like that at first. They didn't think Earl was good for Mom simply because of his age. Some people didn't even give him a chance. On the other hand, some people didn't like Mom for Earl. It turns out that didn't matter because it didn't look like he was going anywhere. He continued to come by every week, multiple times. Gram later told me that she expressed gentle concern to Gramp, as moms often do, about Earl at first. She wasn't sure about this new relationship in her daughter's life. Gramp looked her directly in the eyes and said, "What are we going to do, Hun? She is thirty-eight years old, smart, and beautiful. She can and will certainly make her own decisions. We can either support her like we always have, or we can hold resentment and lose her trust."

Gram responded, "Yeah, I guess you're right."

Just six months after Earl came into our lives, we were forced to befriend change yet again. Mom had picked me up from soccer practice, and we were in the car on the way home. I was in the front seat, covered in sweat. Delilah and Tim Jr. sat in the back of Mom's minivan. Tim Jr. was still in his car seat. Mom made a pit stop for gas and received a phone call while she pumped it. She stepped a few feet away and answered it. Seconds later, she began to cry. Suddenly, that same feeling in my gut that I felt when Gram picked me up from school the day Dad died returned. I felt in every sense that this was going to be bad. I tried to calm myself so that Delilah and Tim didn't worry. Mom got back in the car, wiped her tears, and drove away from the gas pump.

I waited a minute before I asked her, "Mom, do you have breast cancer?" Her eyes welled with tears as she answered me, "Yes, honey. I do." The pain in my chest was intense. In my throat, I felt a lump. Mom never asked me how I knew, but a few days earlier, I had noticed some paperwork she left on the counter. It was a medical form, and she had checked "right breast." I was decently intelligent for my age and put two and two together that evening.

I was in the fourth grade, Delilah was in second, and Tim

was still in preschool. They didn't hear our conversation, and they were so young that I don't think they were paying attention. Mom told them shortly after and then broke the news to Gram and Gramp. Gramp took it the worst since he had already lost his mother and sister to different cancers. She told the rest of the family, and lastly, she told Earl. It would become the most famous conversation of their relationship and possibly even their lives.

Late one evening, when Earl was over and we had already been put to bed, they went outside to the front porch. Mom told Earl that she had been diagnosed with breast cancer. She added that they had caught it early due to self-detection, but she wasn't sure what to expect. Mom had put so much thought into what to tell Earl and just how to say every word. In her mind, she had already committed to the departure. She had committed to the lie that it would be better for her to go through this alone. I think that's where I got my trait of pushing people away when I am most in need of love and support. After so much hurt, we feel we are used to going through adversity by ourselves, and we don't think we deserve pillars along the way. Mom looked at Earl while the stars shone down from above and said to him, "Just go." A look of confusion transpired across his face. Mom continued, "If you're going to leave, leave now." A long pause followed. Earl was still confused. Mom continued and attempted to clarify, "It's easier this way. Trust me. It is going to be a lot for you to be dragged through this. While the kids and I don't have a choice in the matter, you do. I'm already a single mom, now I have cancer. Just go. It's okay."

Earl's eyes met Mom's and from his soul, he said in the

most self-assured manner, "Catalina, where am I going?"

Chapter 5

Who Ever Said You Need Permission to Borrow Someone's Bike?

I made Rose aware of Mom's diagnosis the following day. Rose went home and told her mom, Mrs. Finnley, who brought over a homemade strawberry shortcake later that day. Mom was so appreciative. Mrs. Finnley had never met my mom, so I was amazed at her incredibly sincere act of kindness. It spoke volumes about the kind of people the Finnleys were. Mom continued to receive an outpouring of love from a lot of people in the Cherish community, especially those at Relentless Glory Catholic Church, where we were parishioners.

Rose was there for me a lot in the coming days and weeks after Mom's diagnosis. One friend like Rose was equivalent to five hundred regular friends. I was surprised to have met a friend of her caliber at such a young age. I knew God had sent her to me. She talked with me and listened wholeheartedly. I found that that was not the case with many people, whether adults or children. She later showed me a playground in her neighborhood behind the cul-de-sac that I never knew about. We met each other there once a day and talked as we swung through the air. The other neighborhood kids played on the playground too and often Rose had at least one or two siblings that would find us there. Rose was such an energetic, adventurous soul. We realized later on that we both played soccer, attended the same church, went to the same elementary school, and our birthdays were almost exactly one month apart. My birthday was December 24th, and Rose's was November 13th.

With our lives aligned pretty closely, I saw a lot of her. In addition to having high energy and a heart for adventure, Rose was the holder of numerous talents and great faith. She had the voice of an angel, and I don't say that lightly. It was no surprise to me that she earned herself the lead in our elementary school's musical. I was in the musical too, but I was in the chorus with all the average singers. She was an athlete if there ever was one. I could outrun her on the soccer field, but I had to give it my all and more. Usually, it was her outrunning me. Rose's house was pretty big and had a tire swing in the back. She would throw herself off it into the air and never managed to get hurt. If she did, she would just wipe the dirt off and be on to the next adventure. She was always outside and always moving.

Her best talent, hijacking bikes, I became acquainted with one random Tuesday afternoon when she came running up the street to my backyard. I didn't even have time to wonder why she was running before she had reached me. Lagging behind her was her older brother Josh. I was just standing outside of my fence holding onto my bike's handles preparing to take a nice ride, when all of a sudden, Rose put her hands on it and speedily declared, "Quick!! Give me your bike!" I hadn't uttered a word before she promptly ripped it out of my hands and was off, my bike gone. As thoughts began to swirl in my head, I yelled, "What are you doing?!" but Rose was long gone. She ditched the paved streets and rode my bike through the grass, dodged houses and fences, and went down the hill by the playground until she was out of sight.

When Josh finally reached me, he was enraged, to put it lightly. "Why would you give her your bike?!" I couldn't tell if he was angrier at me or Rose.

"I'm sorry, but I didn't. She ripped it out of my hands!"

"Well, I hope she doesn't mess it up," Josh remarked.

"Can I ask what happened?"

"It's just been a chore-filled day. Rose got angry when my mom asked her to clean, and then she started fighting with me. She called me a name and then bolted out of the house. Now, here we are."

I did get my bike back, unscathed, and Rose was asked to apologize to me. I wasn't angry at her though. I was just amazed at her spirit…and speed. Life had knocked me down a peg or two, but Rose was a firecracker. It wasn't long after hanging out with her that I started to feel more like myself again. Life would never be boring with Rose Finnley by my side.

Our neighbor, Rob, had been mowing the grass for us since Dad's death. Now that Mom had been diagnosed with breast cancer, he told Mom he didn't plan on stopping anytime soon. He even told Mom that he would "do it until he couldn't," if he had to. He also weed-whacked, which made our yard a lot more pleasant during the summer months. When we returned home from Marly and Zion's house, Rob came over and mowed for close to two hours that evening. My friend Marly's mom, Mrs. Rye, watched us a few days a week so Mom could work over the summer months because she continued to work despite her cancer diagnosis. Marly and I had been in the same preschool class, and Mom and Mrs. Rye became good friends. Mrs. Rye was a stay-at-home mom to Zion, who was Delilah's age, while Marly attended the elementary school next door to my school. On the other days, Aunt Jemma watched us along with Gram. I will always remember the sound of Rob's lawn mower because it sounded of compassion and good deeds.

As Rob finished mowing, Rose ventured over to my house. I cannot recall for the life of me how she ended up stuck in a tree in my backyard that evening, but she did. When she realized she was stuck, she asked me to go get help. Instead of running to get Mom or Earl, I ran to the Finnley's house as fast as I could. I knocked on the door and her little brother Jimmy answered.

I said, "You have to come help me and bring Jed or Josh!"

"What is going on?" Jimmy asked.

All I managed to say was, "Rose is stuck in a tree in my backyard!" before Josh made his way to the door with a smirk on his face.

"What did you just say?" he asked cunningly.

"I said...Rose is stuck in a tree, and someone needs to help! She doesn't think she can get down!"

"Show me where," answered Josh Finnley.

I returned with backup which consisted of Jimmy and Josh. Rose was yelling, "Help me! I really don't know if I can get down!"

Earl ran outside when he heard her yell. "Oh my gosh," he whispered. Josh must've still been mad about the bike incident, or maybe something else, because he was living for her being stuck in this tree like a typical big brother. To make it worse, Tim Jr. had left his toys out in the yard and Josh started to throw bouncy balls at her. This resulted in Rose screaming at the top of her lungs, begging Josh to stop it. Josh laughed while Jimmy looked concerned. I knew at that moment I should've just had my mom or Earl try to help her. It was out of my control now, total chaos. They stopped with the teasing, and she finally got down, slowly but surely. She put one leg down and then the other, climbing down the tree until she got as far as she could. Then, she jumped to Earl, who got her to the ground safely. As soon as both of her feet hit the grass, it was over for Josh.

Chapter 6
July 28, 2007

Earl spent the holidays with us in 2006 and helped us build the most realistic snowman I had ever seen, with a scarf and a carrot nose. Earl was so proud of our lifelike snowman. I will admit, he looked one-of-a-kind. Later that year on Mom's birthday, Earl asked her to marry him. Mom said yes. She explained to me what this next step meant by first asking me if I knew what it meant when a man gave a woman a diamond ring. My response, "That he thought you'd like it?" was apparently incorrect. When it hit me, I ran away to Rose's house. I was such a good kid that if I ever did run away, Mom didn't even worry because she knew I would come back. I hated that being the good kid took away all intrigue. There was no search party for the good kid whose best friend lived three houses away, no news outlets involved, just me having the false idea that I had made some sort of point and Mom being slightly annoyed for an hour. Mrs. Finnley finally told me that I was welcome to stay as long as I wanted, but she would need to tell my mom where I was. I decided it was just better to go back home for the night. I wasn't even sure why I ran away; I think I was just sick of all the changes.

    Mom had decided on her treatment plan of a single mastectomy. Her doctors gave her the option to participate in chemotherapy, and she figuratively beat her head against the wall as she tried to decide if she should endure that or not. When the doctor told her that it "wasn't a guarantee of anything," Mom elected for just the surgery. The surgery was scheduled as was the wedding. Mom's last surgery, which would be reconstruction, was scheduled for early June, and the wedding was in late July. After Mom had her mastectomy, Gram decided to stay for a week to help take care of us while Mom focused on her healing. Earl took a few days off that week but returned for the rest of the work week since Gram was with us.

When Mom returned to work after her surgery, the company where she and Earl worked was set to have a budget meeting later that day. Mom and Earl had decided not to tell anyone at work that they were dating, not to mention getting married. They just figured it would be easier that way. I don't think anyone expected it because of their age difference and Mom's cancer. They decided between themselves they would drop it on everyone at the meeting, in a rather clever way. At the end of the meeting, the director of the company asked if anyone had any thoughts or questions. Earl raised his hand and said, "Well, I don't have a question. Just a little personal announcement."

Everyone was thrown off. Earl didn't usually speak at meetings. He confessed, "I'm getting married." The company clapped and offered him congratulations. He went on, "I should also let you know that Catalina is getting married too." There was more clapping and more congratulations. Mom and Earl were sneaky. Still, no one had put it together. They noticeably thought Earl was just announcing the good news for the both of them. Earl went on a little further, "To each other." The room practically exploded with "OH MY GOODNESS" and "WOW." They had managed to keep it a secret from all but two people, Mom's boss, Gayle, and the guy Earl beat to ask Mom out. They were clearly two honest, trustworthy individuals.

Mom and Earl married on July 28, 2007, at Relentless Glory Catholic Church in Cherish, Virginia. The reception took place one street over from Linsell Lane at a modest venue. Earl DJed his wedding reception. Gramp walked Mom down the aisle, Aunt Natalie was Mom's maid of honor, Delilah was a flower girl, Tim Jr. was the ring bearer, and I was a junior bridesmaid. Earl's daughter, Tiffany, was a bridesmaid, and his brother, Benny, was his best man.

Marly's dad, Mr. Rye, gifted Mom and Earl the photography for the day, which he provided himself. Aunt Natalie's husband, my Uncle Colt, managed Earl's DJ equipment so that Earl could enjoy his special day. The only malfunction of the whole day had to do with me and my terrible luck, even at age 11. The security tag was left on the dress I had gotten for the wedding. I did not realize this until an hour before the ceremony, and the store was an hour away. We wouldn't have had time to take it to a local store to get it removed either. There simply wasn't enough time. Someone had the stupidest idea ever to try to yank it off, and one of the adults in my life went for it. I stood in the background cringing when this caused purple ink from the tag to bleed down the right side of my dress. That's why you're not supposed to yank on those…I had to walk down the aisle with my right arm glued to my side to cover the purple ink. No one knew, but Gram was adamant that she would bring it back to the store and let them have a piece of her mind.

Mom was so happy and in love that day, she didn't show

any sign of worry about my dress, or the fact that someone very important to her hadn't shown up. My Uncle Dallas did not attend Mom and Earl's wedding; he is not easily understood. I had only seen Uncle Dallas a handful of times in my life, but still, I felt he should've been there. I never did get around to asking Uncle Dallas if he regretted not attending Mom and Earl's wedding. I would imagine so, but I can't speak to that. I've tried to imagine how it would feel to know that my brother *chose* not to attend my wedding. I can't even imagine. My Mom and Uncle Dallas were extremely close growing up, and he used to come to all my birthday parties...but somewhere along the line that changed. I didn't understand why as I had never heard there had been a huge blow-up. I knew I wasn't privy to all the knowledge; I was just a kid. The old photographs of him next to Mom and Aunt Nat looked so sweet. I knew how much my mom loved her brother, and she forgave him for not being there on that July day in 2007. Mom inspired me, and it hurt my heart to see such a separation in my family. I hoped quietly that it would change.

"It is my pleasure to introduce to you, Mr. and Mrs. Earl Rhoades!" read Uncle Colt. The room erupted with cheer. Rob and Poppy along with Dewdrop were there. Many of the Haughmans had attended. Dad's childhood best friend Bowie was there with his family. It turned out that Bowie's wife, Beverly, had started working with Mom and Earl a few months prior. It was a small world. Unfortunately, in the months leading up to the wedding, our former neighbors Mrs. Hazelton and Dewdrop's husband, Eli, passed away. Rob made sure to get Dewdrop out on the dance floor to cheer her up. Earl had all the true wedding classics ready to play.

Mom and Earl were set to honeymoon in Jamaica for a week at an all-inclusive resort. Mom had made arrangements for me to stay with Aunt Luna, Uncle Max, and our cousin Blair. Delilah was staying with Aunt Jemma, Uncle Crew, and our cousins Catherine and Kelsey. Tim Jr. was staying with Uncle Dane, Aunt Roxy, and our cousins Avery and Ryan. Looking back, the reason we each stayed with a different family member was probably so one person didn't have to care for all three of us plus their kids and so we wouldn't fight. Mom was good. I was just glad Mom was letting us pick who we stayed with. I was even more glad to have Earl Rhoades as my new stepfather.

Chapter 7
Taking The Good with The Bad

The following summer, a few weeks before we were supposed to start middle school, Rose was at her yearly check-up to get the vaccines necessary to enter the sixth grade. It was then her pediatrician noticed a mass on Rose's right hip. Dr. Wales asked Rose about it, and Rose told her she wasn't sure what it was and that she had only started to notice it a few weeks earlier. Dr. Wales then asked her if it had gotten any bigger since she first noticed it. Rose confirmed it had. When Dr. Wales asked her why she didn't share this information with Mr. and Mrs. Finnley, Rose said she was scared and hoped it would disappear on its own. Dr. Wales took all of Rose's information in, observed, did vitals, and tried to remain inconspicuous with her deep concern. She ran blood tests and ordered an x-ray of Rose's hip/pelvis bone. A few days later, Dr. Wales's suspicions were confirmed. Mr. and Mrs. Finnley received a call on July 8, 2008, that stated the unthinkable, that their precious Rose had cancer. They broke the news to Rose later that same afternoon. To say Rose was crushed would be a terrible understatement. Rose knew the second those words fell from her father's lips; her life was never going to be the same.

My mom found out about Rose's diagnosis at church after seeing her name on the prayer list. I hadn't seen Rose outside in a few days, but I had just figured she was busy. Although, I hadn't seen any of her siblings outside either. When my mom told me, I wasn't sure what to think or feel.

I knew I was going to be respectful and give Rose all the time she needed for herself, so I stayed away. It was a lonely rest of the summer, and I found out that Rose would not be in attendance with me at Wildflower Park Middle School. I wondered what a wildflower park would be without a Rose. Mr. and Mrs. Finnley decided it was best if Rose was homeschooled during her sixth-grade year so that she could make treatment the center of her attention. This paired with the news of Rose's diagnosis created some iffy speculations in my mind about how middle school would treat me.

Mom was persistent in the weeks after the news. She asked me every day if I had spoken to or seen Rose yet. My sigh along with my "No, not yet" would tell her everything she needed to know, which was that I hadn't seen Rose since our elementary school's talent show at the end of fifth grade.

"I think you should call her," Mom suggested. So, I did. I dialed her home phone number and Mrs. Finnley answered. I asked if I could please speak to Rose and Mrs. Finnley called out, "Rosie! It's for you." Rose answered and all I could manage was a "Hi." I decided not to ask her *how* she was doing, but rather *what* she was doing. She said she was playing with a xylophone she had found in Jamie's room. I was impressed and could hear her smacking it pretty hard with the mallets. We talked about little things until she brought up the dreaded word. It wasn't fair for someone to have cancer as a child, or ever, but especially as a child. It was tremendously unpleasant for it to happen to a little girl like Rose Finnley. As if I needed another reason to believe life wasn't fair. I had already seen so many of them. I found it interesting that when Mom was diagnosed at thirty-eight, people called her young. I wondered what those same people would say about Rose.

There was a research hospital about an hour from Cherish where Rose would start chemotherapy. The plan was to attempt to shrink her tumor before she could have surgery to remove the rest of it. It was the same hospital where Mom had had her mastectomy. I was worried about Rose, but she came from two parents of great faith. She was the best student in our Sunday school class and loved God. She was a fighter even back when she temporarily stole my bike to get away from Josh Finnley. I had to tell myself that she was going to be okay. It didn't take long for my mom to realize that I was pretty much lost at school without Rose. I was incredibly introverted as a kid, so my mom did what any good mom would do. She talked. A lady she worked with named Penny had a daughter my age. It turned out she went to Wildflower Park Middle too. Mom told me about this, and I just looked at her. What did she expect me to do, go up to this girl and say, "Hi, my mom said to find you and talk. She works with your mom. I know you don't know me from Adam, but I think we should be friends." I asked Mom just that with a little bit of an attitude. Mom put her hands on her hips and said "Seriously, Pia?" I had a blank expression on my face until Mom said, "I talked to Penny, and we decided we would meet up at the mahket so you could introduce yourselves to one anotha."

Her Massachusetts accent frequented the scene when she was…excuse my language…sick of my shit. I told Mom that I would do that, but deep down I didn't expect it to go anywhere.

My mom parked the car at the supermarket and started to look for Penny's car. Her flip phone started to ring. "Oh, it's Penny!" Mom informed me. Penny gave Mom directions to where they were so we could find them. The market in Cherish was vast as it began as the only grocery store in town, so it would have been a long walk without proper details. I walked down the parking lot with Mom until we saw Penny and her daughter, Raven Solace. We were walking down the row that they were walking up. I didn't know it was them until Mom and Penny started waving to each other. Raven had jean shorts on with a T-shirt and had dark, curly hair. I had no idea as I stood in that parking lot on that hot summer day that the daughter of my mom's colleague, who I met in a grocery store parking lot, would become one of my best friends.

Rose joined Raven and me at Wildflower Park Middle School for seventh and eighth grade. Rose had a plan due to her cancer that helped the school administrators and teachers know how to best accommodate her needs, so she could receive a public education just like everyone else. Part of that plan was having a helper to and from class since a surgery Rose had undergone after chemotherapy left her needing to use loft strands to get around. They were pink. I got to be Rose's helper and carry her books for her from class to class. The best part about it was that Rose and I got to leave class five minutes early to do so. It came in handy if we were in math class. It also gave me and Rose time to chat and be silly. Our middle school was two floors, so sometimes Rose had to take the elevator to her next class. We loved to press all the buttons and try to get in before the doors closed, resulting in me almost getting crushed in the door one time.

When I talked to Rose about the most difficult parts of having cancer so young, she told me it was the huge change it brought to just about every area of her life. She could no longer play sports like she enjoyed, she couldn't run around and play outside as well as she used to, it took away her long hair and made people stare at her, but most of all, it made people treat her differently. She could have lived without that. She told me often how she was still the same Rose that people knew before she had Ewing's. She so deeply wished that she could have enjoyed the little things like running down the soccer field or through the yard for the remainder of her childhood. The thing I admired about Rose was despite her entire life changing before her eyes, she remained at peace within. She didn't worry about what would happen. She simply trusted.

She did have moments where she questioned why this had to happen to her, but she understood she would never truly know why it happened to her and promised herself to make the best of it. She gave so much to others even though she was sick, and she was the best friend ever.

Rose still had to miss days here and there to attend treatments. She had started going to treatments at a new hospital after the hospital here had run out of options. Mr. Finnley found a research drug online and brought up the idea to doctors at this hospital in Maryland. They went for it, and it worked so well for her. She was almost cancer free.

Meanwhile, Mom and Earl had put an offer on a house about fifteen minutes outside of town. Delilah, Tim, and I loved the house; I couldn't deny that. It was definitely out in the country, which would be a change since I had only ever lived right in town. It was on a private gravel road with only five houses in total. It rested on four and a half acres, three of which included a patch of magical woods. It was surrounded by winding roads and gorgeous hills. I told Rose about it, and she didn't want me to move, but she wanted me to be happy. She said she would miss me if we did move. I reassured her that I wouldn't be far.

The owners accepted our offer on the house, and we moved to a subset of Cherish called Ralley in mid-October. Our current neighbors Dewdrop, Rob, and Poppy were sad to see us go. Rob said we were moving to "bear country." He wasn't wrong because the first week at the new house, we saw multiple bears. I heartily reminded them that Linsell Lane would always be my true home, and we would be returning often. Halloween arrived and Linsell Lane was the first place we trick-or-treated, and then I went through the entirety of Rose's neighborhood. Rose gave out candy since she was recovering from another surgery. A few weeks later, Rose told me she was in remission.

The Ralley house was white with blue shutters, a gray roof, and a split foyer when Mom and Earl first bought it. Mom had a vision for it, though. She put us to work painting the shutters black and the front door red. We also had to paint the lower half of the back of the house where the siding stopped and the same blue color as the shutters began. I remember despising whoever had painted the back of the house blue. There was also a red deck and a sunroom out back, which Mom loved. She filled the sunroom with gentle decor and a chair. Part of the backyard was fenced off. It was as if we had two backyards because outside of the fence was just…the rest of our yard and the woods. Mom planted two peony bushes in the front yard that she took the utmost pride in. Peonies were her favorite flower. They had a short life span, but when they were here, they were fluffy beams of utter beauty.

Inside the house, the alternating pink and blue carpet that Mom and Earl planned to replace, and the old, stained wallpaper of the kitchen were all quite noticeable. Other than that, there wasn't much to fix upstairs. The basement had thin brown carpet covering a cement floor. When we first moved in, I took the room in the basement since it came with a bathroom that I wouldn't have to share. Delilah's and Tim's rooms were upstairs across from Mom and Earl's room. The dealbreaker about my room was the storage room in it. It made this awful noise that sounded like a dog panting. During the day, the noise wasn't so bad. At night, it kept me up, and it was scary when it was dark. So, after I had moved all my stuff in…and Delilah had moved all of hers upstairs…we switched rooms. It took an entire day. I was so thankful she didn't mind switching. She was braver than I was when it came to noises, darkness, bugs, and many other things.

The neighbors next door had children about our age, and we played with them often. They had 2 daughters older than me, a daughter in between me and Delilah, a daughter younger than Delilah, and a son a few years younger than Tim Jr. A few years later, a new family moved into the last house on the street. They had two young boys who were both younger than the three of us with another one on the way. Delilah and Tim Jr. spent a lot of time outdoors playing with our neighbors' children. I would sometimes talk with our neighbor's older daughters and occasionally play with Delilah and the girl around her age, but usually, I just spent time by myself. Tim loved to play with the other little boys on the street.

    We had one year unscathed by life while living at the Ralley house. It was one of those years that would be hard to beat. It gave me a much-needed sense of normality and stability, two things I hadn't had much of in my little life. I remember Earl opening the garage in the summer and playing music as he and Mom sat there drinking beer while Delilah, Tim, and I played in the front yard. Mom would laugh her joyous, life-giving laugh, and all was good in my life. In the winter, we would sled down the big hill in the backyard on boogie boards that Mom had saved from vacationing at Aunt Jemma's beach house. Our neighbor's kids came out to sled too, and then we used their backyard to extend the sledding path. Once every spring Mom would run into town to get pansies and plant them in the front garden, lining the walkway to the front door. In the fall, Earl would rake up the leaves in the front yard and watch as my siblings and I had way too much fun crashing into the piles. There was also the time Delilah, and I snuck sodas into our bras as Mom was getting home so we could have one. Mom didn't allow us to drink soda unless it was a special occasion, but it was okay for her to have a soda every day. We were home alone for a few minutes, and we decided we were going to take a few of Mom's beloved sodas. Mom wouldn't know. She couldn't. As we were in the garage grabbing them, the garage door started to open. I yelled to Delilah, "Quick! It's Mom!" She yelled, "Shove them in your bra! Run!" I don't think Mom ever figured it out. I appreciated Delilah because not only had she helped me steal a soda that day, but she also ate my broccoli as a kid, so I didn't have to. Those were both much needed.

Mom and Earl took us on a few trips to this darling cottage they found near Earl's marina. It was on a creek connecting to the larger bay. It was the perfect-sized cottage for the five of us. It was peaceful and extremely secluded, so much so that the first time we stayed there, Mom and Earl almost couldn't find it because the front of the home was covered completely by trees. Out back there was a dock where Delilah, Tim, and I would jump off to swim. At one point, Mom saw the three of us standing perfectly on the dock. She screamed from the screened-in porch, "Wait!!!" We all paused and looked behind us. She continued, "Hold still. This is the perfect photo." She was walking quickly to us, camera in hand. She told the three of us, "Hold hands." We complied, and she snapped the photo. This photo would be placed in a frame and displayed in our home. It sat at the top of the stairs and reminded me of happiness each time I passed it.

Life must've remembered it had left us unbothered because it came back with a vengeance. One day, we were at the market with Mom. A day that felt normal to me at the time would become the downfall of my family. What I didn't know was for an instant while we were there, Mom lost sight of everything around her. It went dark. Her vision ended up coming back a few moments later, and she got us home safely, but it was scary for Mom. Raven's mom, Penny, told me many years later that when Mom arrived to pick me up from their house later that same day, Mom "knew it was back" and "knew it was in her brain." Penny was also a woman of strong faith who had been tested and told Mom not to think like that, that it was going to be okay.

Mom said, "Penny...I just know." I must've been twenty-five when Penny finally told me that story. As I sat there listening to her tell me this painful recollection of my mom, I remembered being in the car looking through the window at Mom standing on their steps talking to Penny that very day. I just had no idea what they were saying.

Halfway through my sixth-grade year, Mom found out that she was right. She usually was, but this was a time I wanted her to be vastly wrong. Her cancer was back. Only this time, it had spread to her brain, liver, and lungs. Finding that out felt like someone was giving me advanced notice that I needed to take whatever hope I had left at that point in my youth and chuck it straight into the Chesapeake Bay. There it would surely sink to the bottom where it would soundly rest for the remainder of eternity. It was a random day shortly after this when Mom handed me a pair of scissors and took a seat on the pink carpet in the hallway upstairs. "Do it. It's okay," she said as she held out a strand of her long, highlighted hair. Mom had thick, gorgeous hair. I began to cry. Mom picked up the scissors and told me I didn't have to do it, but that I could give her any haircut I wanted. It was going to fall out anyway. I stood there for a second deciding if I wanted to cut her hair or if I wanted to let it fall out on its own. The only reason I decided to take the plunge was because I wanted to try to make Mom a wig accessory for her hat. I gave her a shoulder-length cut and then took her hair into my room. My precious little heart thought I could hot glue my mom's hair to the back of her favorite baseball cap. She loved to wear hats, so it was the sweetest gesture. When it didn't work, I kept her hair, brought Mom her hat back, and apologized. Then, I cried some more. Mom smiled and said, "It's really okay." I would watch the rest of it fall out and notice pieces of her hair in the shower for weeks. I remember being at the bus stop at the end of our gravel road with Delilah shortly after finding out Mom's cancer had returned. I whispered to her, "Don't tell" when our neighbors opened their door to join us. She said softly back to me "I know, I won't." We didn't want people to know until it was time for them to know.

If you don't remember when you were in middle school, you don't have kids, or your kids haven't reached that age yet, let me educate you a little. Middle school is naturally one of the most crucial and sensitive times for adolescents. They are becoming young adults, going through puberty with a surge of various hormones, and figuring out who they are. It's called middle school for a reason. It truly stands as the middle between a person's early childhood and late childhood years. It's supposed to be a training ground, and it's supposed to be rough. It was even more rough and terrible for me. I had absolutely no idea how to navigate the world of puberty, my mom's metastatic cancer, and the everyday drama in the world of a middle school girl. I was, to put it lightly, a hot mess. I remember having outbursts for a while. I was angry from time to time. Understandably so. I was angry that my mom was sick, angry that I didn't have my dad. I was just angry at the world and everyone in it. I got angry at God, too. Eventually, my outbursts stopped, and I was back to being the good kid. I felt something had changed in me, though. I couldn't place it. We now call that anxiety, and I think this was where it started.

I would walk the halls of middle school as a little middle

school girl, each day my posture tipped more and more downward, as if a large boulder sat on the center of my back. If you observed me from the outside, besides the bad posture and the fact that I looked rather timid, you probably wouldn't have been able to tell there was anything majorly wrong with me. On the inside, the waves were ceaseless against the walls of my chest. I worried about Mom all day at school. I worried about her no matter what, especially when I knew she had chemotherapy or a procedure. Things started out relatively hopeful with the doctors, despite how hopeless the situation sounded when she found out.

Mom had seven lesions in her brain and would need to start radiation along with intensive chemotherapy for the other areas of her body with cancer. I remember very little about my actual middle school experience. Much of what I remember about middle school consists of my friends, Rose and Raven, the teachers who made a difference every day, and being in the guidance counselors' offices daily due to worrying or regular middle school drama. I don't remember much else. Somewhere in the midst of all the chaos, Rose's treatment had stopped working for her.

We were trying to do the best we could as middle school girls, with the limited knowledge we had, yet our personal lives were so unfair for our age. Our friendship suffered due to these personal crosses we were forced to carry. I still carried Rose's books when I was mad at her. Our fights were so stupid. Many of them didn't even make any sense. I don't even truly think we were ever mad at each other. I think we were mad at life and took it out on each other. I learned that you only fight that way with those you are extremely comfortable with and close to.

Rose was another sister to me, so it made sense. They were messy years but years that you look back on and stare in awe of your strength and the friendship that surrounded you. Let me not discount the fact that my friends from church and Sunday school and Raven were amazing friends during these years too.

Rose's doctors at the Maryland hospital found another trial drug that Rose qualified for. Because her cancer was so rare, she was often eligible for trials. It was a huge toss-up with a trial drug, and if a person's cancer was aggressive, it was risky to waste time on a slender possibility like a trial treatment. There was limited research about them because they were still trials. There were no guarantees that trial drugs would work at all, let alone how long they would work for if a patient's body took to it. This one, blessedly, appeared to work for her.

Chapter 8
The Fake Finnley and The First First Holy Communion

I will never forget the Sunday after Mom's second cancer diagnosis. I say that because the way she prayed that morning is forever burned into my memory. It was the type of praying that you do from your soul, the cover your face with both hands as you sink away from the physical church building. I knew what she was praying for. I think everyone in the building did. She knew how serious her illness had become. She knew that she had three young children. She knew she had Earl, the man she loved so much. I have often thought about how my mom felt at that point in her life, and I don't think any words could truly describe it. It was a nightmare for her. I don't have many fears, but one of my biggest ones is one day understanding what she felt that day. I hope I never do. No mom ever deserves to feel that way.

I have failed to comprehend how my mom's cancer went from "remission" to "metastatic." It did not make sense to me. My guess was when she had her surgery, they missed just a single cell. A single, tiny, unseen cell was the difference between a happy life and the nightmare we found ourselves in. It's possible that that wasn't the case. I would never truly know. It was ultimately the most unfortunate circumstance of my life. I found out later on that the brain is breast cancer's favorite place to spread to. Cancer is truly horrific. Due to my life, I've struggled with consistency in many areas. Prayer has been one. I should always be practicing my faith because it's a lifelong journey, not one where you get to a certain level and can stop. I do think that even when I am far away from Jesus, I still do a good job of keeping Him in my mind and heart. I don't want this book to be something where you feel like you can't relate if you aren't religious, or you don't know where you stand with God. I want this to be a book you feel good about reading, no matter who you are or what your background is. We all go through adversity, not just Christians. I just wanted to say that faith, the Christian faith, makes sense out of the deepest pain and suffering. It implants in you a little light that shines through the darkness when you feel distraught and completely alone. It's made the greatest difference for me despite my struggle to maintain a consistent prayer life.

There are Christians out there who ruin it for the rest of us. The bad ones are sometimes the loudest. They do so much harm, and those are the ones people seem to share on social media to label all Christians, which is equally as harmful as the bad Christians to begin with. On the other side of that, there are so many Christians I look up to, Christians who live lives that inspire. We call those the real ones. Mom was one of the real ones. She was not one of those people who would drag a non-believer even further away from God. I think Mom's faith spoke volumes and inspired many people she encountered. She bonded with Gayle, Penny, Mrs. Finnley, and many others due to her faith.

In addition to processing the return of her cancer, Mom questioned herself for not originally doing chemotherapy. My heart truly broke when I found that out. Earl assured me that her doctor was the best one she could have had, one he greatly trusted. This doctor told Mom that even if she had done chemotherapy the first time around, her cancer could have still come back. That helped her. My mom trusted in God's goodness even when she didn't understand the life circumstances she found herself in. I greatly admired that quality about her. Mom believed wholeheartedly that God was good, but God being good did not mean bad things would not happen. I remember her saying many times, "If Jesus had to go through what He went through, why would I think I'd be free from suffering?" or something to that effect. So many Christians, me included, struggle with God allowing bad things to happen to us and our families. Father Mike Schmitz tells us, "His perfect will is that He brings about a greater good, even through stuff that we just don't get, even through death, even through accidents, even through disease, and that should give us hope." I will always remember how Mom remained so trusting when most of her world was pitch black. I will never forget her glow of hope. I don't know if I could have been so positive. She wanted so badly to live. She wanted to watch her children grow up. She wanted to guide them, watch them graduate high school and college, attend their weddings, and one day become a grandma. That was a lot to look forward to, so she wasn't planning on going out without a fight. My mom was one hell of a woman.

 Mom permitted me to accompany Rose several times to treatment in Maryland. One time it was Mrs. Finnley who drove us to the hospital. Most of the time, it was Mr. Finnley who took Rose to treatment. There was so much security to go through to get into this hospital because it was one of the country's largest research hospitals. We each had to sign in when Mr. Finnley pulled up to the window. He said our names to the security woman, and she printed badges for us. Mr.

Finnley handed us our badges. Joshua Finnley, Rose Finnley, and Pia Finnley. I held my badge in my hand and pondered over the 'Pia Finnley'. Should I let Rose or her father know my badge was wrong? Was it going to get me in trouble for illegal entry to the hospital? They would know when they saw me wearing it, so I decided to speak up.

"Uh, there's a small problem. It's fine, but I wanted to say something," I said aloud.

"What's up?" Mr. Finnley asked.

"My badge is wrong. I mean, my first name is right, but my last name is wrong."

Mr. Finnley's interest peaked when he continued, "What last name does it say?"

I responded "It says Finnley. Pia Finnley."

Mr. Finnley looked at Rose and me through his rearview mirror and said something I'll never forget. He said, "That's okay. Looks like you're sisters now," and drove into the parking garage.

It was an honor to be Rose Finnley's unbiological sister.

We usually had multiple doctors to see, which took most of the day. The pediatric unit was the most colorful and where the nurses happened to be the nicest. I always listened when I was there to make sure I knew Rose's full medical situation. Mr. Finnley asked introspective questions to the doctors. I could tell Rose was in the best care, both in the hospital and at home. We ran into one of Rose's friends from the summer camp she attended regularly. The camp was for children with cancer. Cora was so friendly and had the bubbliest personality. I was glad to have met her but felt my heart break a little for her and all she had gone through. Cora was on the upswing, though. She was soon to be done with all treatment and scheduled for follow-ups only. I was so happy for her.

When we got back to the Finnley's house, Rose and I took a walk to the lake in the neighborhood next to Rose's and just talked. It was only about a fifteen-minute walk, and the area had a playground, a path for running or walking, and a clearing beside the lake. The clearing left just enough space for us to sit down next to each other and enjoy the view along with each other's company. There was a sign next to the lake that read "NO SWIMMING." I asked Rose if she thought I'd get in trouble if I swam in it. She pointed at the sign and shook her head.

We only spent half an hour at the lake because I knew Mom was on her way to get me. Mr. Finnley and Mrs. Finnley directed the choir at Relentless Glory Catholic Church and had practice later that evening. Rose sang in the children's choir and kept harping on me to join. The Finnleys were blessed with numerous talents, singing being their best one. Acting was a close second. I would sometimes sit with Rose at church, and I never told her this, but I would sometimes only pretend to sing because I couldn't possibly meet their level of tunefulness. Rose said she thought I had a decent singing voice, and maybe I did, but I definitely needed a lot of voice coaching to feel like I could fit in with the Finnleys at church. No one would be confusing me for a Finnley at a concert or in the church pew.

As we entered the eighth grade, Mom continued to fight

with her heart and soul. She went through some awful procedures that to this day make my skin crawl. I don't ever see how anyone justified these as humane. As if chemotherapy and radiation didn't leave Mom (and Rose) riddled with many side effects, Mom endured other procedures too. One was known as gamma knife. I won't delve into too much detail, but it involves a type of radiation where they insert a metal helmet into—yes, into—your forehead. They then use precise "gamma" rays to radiate specific tumors or lesions in the brain. This left Mom with two scars on her face and likely other side effects she did not disclose. I heard Mom admit once that if it had been up to her, she'd have already quit a long time ago. She was doing this for us, and that left me with a feeling both sweet and sour. She wanted to watch us grow up. I'm not sure if gamma knife ever shrunk any of Mom's lesions or helped make any positive progress, but I imagine it did a little.

    Mom had the most aggressive form of breast cancer known as triple negative. While Mom was a feisty little Bostonian, it didn't help that her cancer was quite feisty too. I heard Mom on the phone once with a doctor at an institution in Boston. She wanted to get a second opinion to make sure she was following the right steps. Earl and Mom even took a trip to Boston to meet this doctor in person. After careful review, the doctor assured Mom that her doctors in Virginia were doing everything right. Life continued to forge on in spite of Mom's cancer. Tim Jr. was set to make his First Holy Communion later next year, but Mom worried about her health and this important moment in Tim's faith journey. Mom decided to talk to Father Theo one fall afternoon. Father Theo was a special priest and a man who had grown close to our family. He was from Holland and was "accidentally" shipped to the United States. It was always so wild to me that he ended up here by accident and just stayed. In the small town of Cherish of all places. I'm not sure all of the details on that...but it's kind of hilarious that the bishop in charge just said, "Mix up...but you know what...why don't we just see how this one goes?" I'm being facetious. Father's story just goes to show that God sends people where they need to be, and His plan is always the best.

Father Theo was the first pastor of Relentless Glory. He married Mom and Earl, baptized Delilah and Tim, and was there for both Delilah's and my First Holy Communions. Mom had confided in him over the years on many occasions. She went to see him that fall afternoon first and foremost to update him on her health prognosis. He prayed with Mom and over her. She then told him how Delilah and I were doing. Lastly, she made a request. Father Theo accepted Mom's request to have Tim make his First Holy Communion a few months early during a regular Sunday mass to ensure Mom would be able to be there for it. It was a wonderfully special day for Tim and our family.

Mom continued to fight in the months and weeks that followed. Things started to progress, though. Mom stayed the course, for us. I remember so many little things. I remember Mom at Tim Jr's football games, cheering for him from the sidelines despite her being as sick as she was. I looked over at her and thought about how I hoped Mom could keep doing this in the years to come, but that if she couldn't, I hoped Tim knew how much Mom loved him. She had so much fun watching him play.

Knowing Mom was sick made me replay memories with her in my mind. My mom was such a good mother. She bought a laptop when I was around the age of twelve. It was the first laptop my family ever owned. We had a computer when we were younger and lived on Linsell Lane, but it was truly a dinosaur. We were so excited when my mom bought it, and so was she. We always had everything we needed, but we were never rich. It took my mom so long to pay that laptop off. She was so happy when she finally did. One day, I was playing on the laptop and drinking a ginger ale when it happened. I spilled the ginger ale all over her laptop. It sunk in underneath the keyboard, and everything became so sticky. I tried to get a towel and dry it off, but it was too late. I told my mom, who must've seen the sadness in my eyes because I did understand how hard she worked to get it for us. She looked at me and just said, "It's okay, Pia. I'll set it in the sunroom so it can dry off." She never yelled, scowled, or anything close to that. I was amazed at how calm she was. It would have been so easy for her to scream. I would have wanted to had I been in her shoes. She most likely understood that if she had reacted that way, it would have upset me for so much longer than she would have been upset about the laptop. In an instant, she chose to not leave me with a bad memory, and deal with the frustration by herself. That is one moment I will always remember. I still feel bad about her laptop, but I learned so much from my mom. I hope to be able to address situations with my kids one day in the same gentle manner no matter how angry I may be.

We visited places where people stared at Mom. It was like they had never seen a person with cancer. It made me so angry. I wanted to look at them and say, "What??? Is there a problem?" but I didn't because I knew the type of person my mom had raised me to be. One place we visited while Mom was sick was an amusement park on the other side of the state. My great-aunt had bought us this trip so that we could enjoy ourselves with Mom and not have to worry about anything. I pushed Mom in a wheelchair, and I remember one lady saying, "That's so sweet," to her friend. I had this intense awareness that my life as I knew it was slipping away, and the only thing I could do was tell it to be careful on the way out.

Some of the other changes I remember we faced were little things like Mom eventually couldn't be around really loud noises due to her brain lesions. I remember she couldn't go into the skating rink due to the loud music and endless flashing lights. There were so many other small changes we had to make, and each one was like inching closer to the harsh reality of how serious her illness was. I often looked at Mom with her scarf and hat on and thought about how much I loved her. I never told her that I looked at her from time to time and reflected, but I did. Mom had no hair, no eyelashes, and scars on her face from gamma knife radiation. I overheard Mom on the phone one day talking to Aunt Luna. She had called to check on Mom and see if she needed anything. Mom said, "Oh, thank you, Luna. I'm actually great. I don't have to shave my legs or put on mascara. Showers are quicker than ever!" I was amazed at Mom finding the silver lining in her awful disease. She still smiled deeply, still laughed, still made the best of it. She was the bravest woman I knew.

I should mention that Gramp died a few months prior. It was terrible for Gram. She loved Gramp with her heart and soul. In addition to Mom being sick, this put Gram through the wringer. I always feel bad when I think about this because I was young and couldn't be there for my Gram in the capacity she needed. She ended up having to sell her house, move into a tiny apartment, and sell or donate so many of her cherished belongings. She also had to continue to help care for Mom without the support of her husband. She was also an incredibly strong woman. There was no coincidence in that. I am thankful for one thing that came from the loss of Gramp. I am thankful that I was given the chance to watch how my mom handled the loss of a parent. It wasn't the same as when I lost my father. Mom was an adult and sick with cancer. I was a child. Nonetheless, it may sound strange, but as a young girl, I observed how the adults in my life handled pain. She had to grieve the loss of her father while being so sick. I know this was not a realistic example of grief, but Mom handled it with more grace than I can even describe. She didn't stumble. She couldn't. There was too much at stake. I knew she was hurting but watching her carry on was such a gift. It's helped me on the hard days. Knowing she carried on with her head held high reminded me that I could too.

Chapter 9

The Loneliest Days in 2010

It was a mid-October afternoon in 2010 when Mom sat us down at the dining room table after school and did the most excruciating, heartbreaking thing she ever had to do. The doctors had exhausted all options. Mom's cancer was simply too aggressive, and research did not show any other alternatives for Mom at this time. They gave her two to three months. She told us, "This is the hardest thing I have ever had to tell my three children," as she looked at Earl and held back her tears. I could visibly see the despair on her face. She had given it her all, and we knew that. Mom continued, "I want you to know how much I love you. I'm so sorry." The fact that she apologized to us was what broke my heart. Why was *she* sorry? I felt sorry for her first and foremost. No mother should ever have to go through telling her children that. As Mom told us this terrible truth, I felt in my gut that I knew it had all been too good to be true. I knew that this was where we'd end up. I was so negative, and I hated that I was usually right.

The next three months were the strangest and most emotionally draining months of my entire life. I was thirteen, and I was only in the 8th grade. I knew I was about to lose the only biological parent I had left. That sucked. I felt so many things, but I didn't know what to do with them or who to tell. I couldn't tell Mom, and all the other adults in my life were swept up in their own grief, and rightly so. They were about to lose their daughter, wife, sister, or beloved friend.

Mom was the one I wanted to tell the most. I wanted to cry in her arms like a baby, but I just knew I couldn't burden Mom with *my* pain. I couldn't imagine how Mom felt, and this wasn't the first time in my life I had felt like this. How did it feel to know she was going to die? To have to say goodbye to her three children? To the man she loved so much? To her mom? To her sister and brother? Mom was only forty-one. She had so much life left to live. I pondered these things. My heart shattered for Mom.

The one blessing to be found in the horrible evil that was cancer was that it gives you the ability to recognize the value in time. Not only to recognize it but to utilize it to your advantage. We were able to make the most of the two to three months we had left. You can accomplish a lot in that amount of time when you put your mind to it. We went on one last trip with Mom, and I got to miss a day of school to go. Mom sat down with Gram and listed out all her wishes for us in the order in which she preferred them. Her first choice was for us to stay with Earl in our house and attend the same schools. Her second choice was for us to live with her sister, Auntie Nat, who lived locally. Her third choice, I believe, was for us to go with Gram. She did not want us to be separated. She wanted us to remain close to the Haughman family, and she told me that many times. She wanted us to keep going to church and Sunday school. She wanted her three children to remain close. She hoped we would always refer to her and only her as "Mom" despite the lack of time we got to spend with her. That last one broke me.

Mom was also able to write us each a letter, which we would be given once she died. Her fine motor skills had started to go, so she typed them on Gram's computer and signed them.

They also came with a picture of Mom on her honeymoon in Jamaica only three short years ago with text over it that read, "I Love You, Mom, <3" and a short, handwritten note on the back. The picture displayed Mom sitting on the edge of a water fountain looking as gorgeous as ever. Mom had lunch with Gram for a few weeks where they talked about her life and her wishes in detail. I'm sure other things came up too. Mom told Gram, along with many others, "Pia will be fine. She's level-headed, and I'm not worried about her. Same with Tim. Delilah, though. You will all need to watch out for her. She is a rebel. She's going to keep you on your toes." No one knew what Mom meant at the time, but out of the three of us, Mom knew she would be the one to visibly struggle.

I remember the last Halloween I had with Mom. We always trick-or-treated on Linsell Lane and then went over to Rose's neighborhood. I sat in the car with Mom in front of Dewdrop's house on the very street I had called home for so long. I wanted Mom to go with me to Dewdrop's door, but she didn't want to. I kept prodding her, saying, "Come on. I'm sure she wants to see you." Mom snapped at me and said, "Do you think I really want to go in there and tell her how sick I am?!" She was on the verge of tears, and I felt bad for even suggesting it. It was a kick to my chest, to say the least. I hated reality checks. I held back my tears so hard on Halloween night in 2010.

Hospice started to come a few weeks later. The decline was slow, and so was hospice at first. I hated that the hospice nurse we were assigned was the mom of a girl I went to school with. Even though this woman's daughter was a year older than me and in high school now, I just felt uncomfortable about it. The nurse ended up being super nice, so I got over it. Hospice would check on Mom and bring supplies. Gram and Earl were instrumental parts of Mom's comfort to the very end. They held her hand and provided various amounts of comfort for her. The things they did for her were no doubt hard for them to do but done out of pure love for her. I remember the first few weeks not being able to notice a change in Mom. As the weeks went on, Mom was on a good amount of pain medicine, so she started to hallucinate. She said strange things like she had pots and pans on her walls, or that a cat had gotten into her room. She asked me if I would get the pots and pans off her wall. Before she had gotten sick, she was particular about the cleanliness of her house, so I thought it was kind of special in a way that even when she was on these high-dose medications, she still kept a little bit of herself close by. I decided to go along with it because it was the last little bit of life I had left with my mom. I told her that I would take the pots and pans down, and I apologized for the cat. I remember her saying to me, "It's okay," as I cried silently in the background.

 I don't think hospice truly knew what the timeline was as far as how much time we had left with Mom. They tried to give us one, but cancer was so unpredictable. They kept saying things like "It won't be much longer." They didn't know because if they did, they wouldn't have said it about 12 times. It didn't take a rocket scientist to figure that out. I remember telling Gram and Aunt Natalie that I didn't want to go to school. I had a feeling in my stomach that felt as though I hadn't eaten in forty-five days. I couldn't focus. I wasn't mentally present to anyone around me. Gram told me I needed to go to school because it would take my mind off what was happening at home. Maybe it did a little, but nothing was truly that powerful. I knew my mom was dying.

Mom's side of the family was Polish, and we had a tradition of gathering at Gram and Gramp's house on Christmas Eve to eat Polish food and go out onto the porch with Gram to look for the first star. Uncle Dallas would be there with his three girls. Everyone was happy. I would've craved to be there versus walking the gravel road from my bus stop to the Ralley house wondering if my mom was still alive. The tiny panic I had when I thought about her not being there made my heart tremble. If you have never witnessed a loved one in hospice care, you may not know that a person's hearing is the last thing to go. A fact I wish I didn't know. I remember the hospice nurse saying to me, "You can talk to her. She can hear you." Gram encouraged me to talk to Mom as often as I felt up to it. Around Thanksgiving, we heard "It won't be much longer," again. Gram said it was time for each of us to go have our "last talk" with Mom.

We set aside time on this random school night to each talk to Mom for as long as we wanted or needed, to say everything we wanted to say. No matter what has come or will come my way in life, nothing will ever feel as insurmountable as that. I felt totally and completely lost when I walked into a room to have the last talk with my dying mom at only age thirteen. There was so much I wanted to say, but I also had so much life to live. I was only thirteen, how was I supposed to know everything I wanted to say to my mom for the rest of my life? I am so proud of myself for doing the best I could. I first told Mom that I loved her and how grateful I was that God picked her to be my mom. I then told her how unfair this was. I went through our favorite memories together and promised to look out for Delilah and Tim. I told her about my dreams in life, such as where I would go to college and that I would name my first daughter Noel. Spoiler alert, I didn't go to this college, but I still do like the name Noel for a daughter. I don't have children yet, but it's no longer my top pick. I think I originally loved it so much because it was Christmas-related.

On December 24, 2010, Rose and Mrs. Finnley took me out to breakfast to celebrate my 14th birthday. They knew the situation going on at home with my mom and wanted to provide some relief for me. We took silly pictures with the menus, and I smiled for the first time in a while. If you were to see the picture of Rose and me that day, you'd never know what was going on in my life at that time. Later that afternoon, my great Aunt Birdie and her husband, Uncle Simeon, took me, Delilah, and Tim to visit Dad's grave. It was likely because things started to look bad, and they wanted to take us out of the house. When we pulled into the cemetery to see Dad, three baby deer crossed in front of the car. Aunt Birdie said, "Look, kids! It's three baby deer! How special. Like the three of you." There were no deer parents in sight. After we had spent time visiting with Dad, we got back in the car to head back home. Aunt Birdie's phone rang before we had even fully made it out of the cemetery. She said, "Uh-huh. Okay. Thank you for calling." I can recall the biggest sniffle from her when she stopped the car, turned around to us, and said, "Sweeties." A pause proceeded. "Your mom went to heaven today."

Rarely we are loved so fiercely that it sets us apart. I consider myself one of the lucky ones to have known unconditional love in this harsh world. In the face of uncertainty, she was unwavering, and in the midst of obstacles that weaken most, she was bold. She had a laugh as breathtaking as autumn and arms as sweet as springtime. She was so overwhelming in her beauty and grace that to know her for thirteen years and one day was somehow enough to last me my entire life but simultaneously not adequate time at all. To know her was to be inspired for the rest of your life and changed all the while. I am filled with wonder having known her.

My mom passed away at 3:18 pm on Christmas Eve of 2010, holding onto Earl's hand. Gram held the other. She passed on my 14th birthday, and two short days before her forty-second. She was taken from this Earth and carried into heaven while we were at the cemetery with my dad. Thinking about that was a depressing kind of beautiful. On the actual Christmas Eve I was born, my birth time was recorded as 2:45 pm. I believe my mom wanted to spend one last birthday with me, so as I've gotten older, I've looked at it less as having terrible luck and more as a blessing. I will say, it doesn't make it any easier to deal with each birthday that has come and gone since then. Losing a parent on your birthday, especially when your birthday is on Christmas Eve, creates the most complex whirlwind of emotions. When it's paired with the fact that I was only fourteen, it makes it even more stormy.

For a while, I wished I could switch my half birthday of June 24th and my real birthday of December 24th. People wouldn't care so much when they ID'd me, it wouldn't get dark at four pm, the list goes on...but there's something special about the parts of our lives that we wish we could change. If your life has been hard, if there's something you desperately wish you could change, or if you are currently going through something difficult, know that you are loved in both the Junes and Decembers of life. You will be okay if you find yourself in the middle or the end. I'm not writing this to claim I have the answers. I don't, but if your birthday is the same day as a loved one's passing or even the week of, I want you to know that you are not alone. My advice would be to look for the positives. What a hypocritical comment coming from a natural-born pessimist like me, but it's the truth. If you tend to think more negatively due to your trauma, it may be a struggle. It still is for me. I have to battle the negatives each year and in the months leading up to it. For a while, I experienced the strangest feeling around the middle of October through the end of December. As time went on, it would just find me on the first of December through the end of the month. I finally saw a doctor who confirmed I was experiencing some PTSD due to my mom's death. I had watched her die. My body knew, my mind knew, and it was reacting.

 Each year when I am in that battle zone, I just think about how lucky I am to share a birthday with my mom. My earthly birthday is her heavenly one. *We were always connected.* It may come with a wave of emotions each year, but my birthday is the day my mom became pain-free. I watched her suffer through agonizing pain, and that would always be worse than my new reality of a hard birthday. The end of this year will mark fourteen years since her passing. I will have had her for just as much time as she's been gone. That's such a difficult reality; however, I've learned to celebrate. There's an old home video of Earl asking Mom what day it was and she said in the happiest, most cheerful voice, "Uhhh! It's

December 24th!" I play that on repeat sometimes. I wish I had the answers. Surround yourself with love, even if it's with one person. Remind yourself that your birthday was chosen for you for a reason. Give yourself a homework assignment of trying to love your birthday more than you hate it. It will take a while, but there's no due date. I can't explain it, but I was meant to have a December 24th birthday. It fits me, and as difficult as it is to watch a parent suffer and die, it makes you understand the importance of a person being at peace. You deserve that same peace on your birthday.

We made it back home from Dad's cemetery before the funeral home had made it to our house. The funeral home my family chose to go with was over an hour away. They had done Dad's and Gramp's services, so they knew our family well. They drove all the way to Ralley on Christmas Eve; they were nice people. I will, unfortunately, always remember so much about my 14th birthday. The December sky wasn't its usual color of gray that day. It was darker. As I stared at the melancholic December sky, my eyes became focused on the bare trees in the distance that lined our gravel road. After I had stared out the window for a while, I remembered sitting on the couch and focusing my eyes on the old pink carpet that Mom and Earl never replaced. I could pick out each string of the carpet. I stared at it until I was forced to blink. I spent half an hour doing this. The next half hour I paced through the house. I stared at the floor while I paced. I remember looking into the mid-afternoon December sky for the second time and thinking about how awful December's company was that day. I wished I could transport back to June or July. Aunt Natalie and Uncle Colt eventually came over and sat on dining room chairs in the living room while

I zoned out into the abyss.

The funeral home finally arrived, and I immediately walked into our front yard. I didn't want to be in the house when they took Mom. I stood by the front door until the funeral home workers picked up Mom's body, placed a white sheet over her, and carried her to the hearse. I looked, but I wish I didn't. I can still picture it all. It was frigid. The type of cold that could cut through your skin. I didn't have a coat on. I just stood there and watched them drive down our gravel road, listening to the crunching of the rocks until I could no longer see the brake lights. A few minutes later, I called Rose. I told her what had happened, and she didn't know what to say. She sent me a message later that night and said Mrs. Finnley was shocked it happened that day of all days.

That night, Mom's slippers sent me into a world of despair. For some reason, all I could do that day was stare at the floor of our house. It felt too burdensome to look anyone in the eyes. The sight of Mom's old slippers in the corner made me realize she would never wear them again. She would never be back in this house. She would never comfort me, Delilah, or Tim ever again. She wouldn't attend my wedding or meet my children. She really had died, and I would never, ever see her again. I was bawling uncontrollable tears. I found Earl and screamed, "Why did this have to happen?!" as tears continued to gush from my face. Earl responded, "I don't know, Pia," so frankly. His answer was so simple that it made me feel truly alone. I hated this for him too. I just wanted my life to go back. I wanted Mom to be here and our family to continue the way it was. We were so happy. It was all so unfair. My tears and I became well acquainted with one another on that Christmas Eve night.

We woke up the next morning on Christmas Day. The gut-wrenching feeling I had that morning was the worst feeling to have on Christmas. Mom had bought all the gifts for us before she died. Earl had wrapped them and put them under the tree. Opening those presents that said 'from Mom' after the previous day was like ripping open a deep, painful wound you had literally just gotten the day before. The pain was so intense. I cried all morning. Delilah and Tim couldn't cry. They just had blank expressions on their faces. Earl stood in the background holding back tears as he watched us open our gifts. Our house was oddly silent. No one said anything after we opened the gifts. There was no, "Oh! Wow! That's just what you wanted, Tim, isn't it?" No "thank yous" because Mom wasn't there to thank. Just a silent opening of gifts and setting them aside until all we could do was look at one another, expressionless. Earl put on Christmas music from Mom's radio that she used to play each Christmas morning. It felt like someone was pouring alcohol onto my wound and the only thing that made it hurt less was the silence wasn't so loud anymore. I feel torn between saying it was a good Christmas because Mom did make it special without even being there and saying that it was one of the worst. Christmas had been so different the year before. There was light and laughter. Now, there was just pain. And somehow, I felt the most for Earl.

We buried my mom four days after Christmas. Mom was buried next to her dad and not mine. It never really bothered me that my parents wouldn't be buried together. I always understood it because I knew Mom wanted to be buried with Earl one day, and she deserved to be. I would just have to get used to not being able to make one trip to visit both of my parents on the hard days. I'd have to make two. I will never forget the church bells ringing through my soul or seeing my friends off in the distance at the cemetery as Mom's burial took place. Rose and Raven were there along with some of my other friends from Sunday school and church.

Everyone wore a pink ribbon that displayed Mom's name. I remember proceeding into the church and reading her eulogy. That's about it. In Mom's eulogy, I spoke of her deep love for coffee, peonies, her favorite football team…but most of all…I spoke about the kind of mother she was. The type of mother everyone who has children should strive to be. I kept it brief but meaningful. There was a small gathering at the hall that belonged to the church after the service and burial. I couldn't smile, and I had dyed my hair a dark brown to match how I felt. Mom's Massachusetts family all came down for the service. Gram's sister was there along with her children. These people were some of the best I had ever known. They loved Mom so much and had grown up with her. There was Aunt Nellie, Aunt Cammie, and Aunt Juniper, who we called Juni. These ladies were not truly my aunts; they were Mom's cousins. We have just always called them aunts, I think, to be respectful. I also think they act like my aunts, so it's appropriate. Mom was only one year apart from Aunt Nellie. I have a few movie scenes in my mind that I can recall from that day, but that's about it. I do remember the feeling of dread and thinking it didn't matter how many people smiled at me or tried to cheer me up. I had a long way to go, in every single way possible. I was only 14. I hadn't even started high school yet. It felt exhausting to think about how much of a mountain I had to climb to get to the rest of my life I had left to live…and that I'd have to do it all without Mom. It felt like a ridiculously tall and unfair task. I also didn't feel like I would be able to do or become much in my life. It felt like the odds were already against me, like my story was already written, and I didn't know if I had any strength left in my frail, fragile body to fight back.

Chapter 10

The Aftermath

Since Mom died over our winter break, I only missed a few days of school due to her passing. I remember returning to school to finish my eighth-grade year in the small town I called home. My feelings juxtaposed against each other made no sense when I tried to describe them, but I knew they were very real. It felt like I was in a huge fishbowl where no one was touching me, yet I also felt like I was being stared down, hard. Everyone knew what had happened to me. I was technically an orphan. My teachers knew. My friends knew. The whole school knew. I was just hoping they would forget soon enough. Then, I would be free to suffer in silence. As an introvert, I liked that way best. When I think about my little eighth-grade self, I want to hug her. I can't even imagine being back in that spot of fresh grief. It was fresher than fresh grief, the worst kind. I was so young, and my adolescent brain was overwhelmed by what had happened to me, not just with my mom, but with both of my parents. It is so crazy when I think about how much I went through so young. Not only did I carry *my* pain, but I worried about my siblings every hour of every day. I never told them, but I think I have always been a mom at heart.

There was this one moment from Mom's passing that lived in my body ever since it happened. I had just gotten home from the grocery store with Gram. Gram was in the kitchen putting groceries away. Earl wasn't home and neither were Delilah or Tim Jr. I went to check on Mom, who was pretty much in and out of it at this point. She could tell I entered the room because she opened her eyes a little and questioned, "Is Timmy here?" My eyes welled with aggressive rivers that fell down my face in the form of tears, but I knew they were more than tears. They were long, detailed letters of my aching soul that my mind could not formulate thoughts for. I asked Mom to repeat what she said even though I knew what she said. I had heard her. She asked me again if Timmy, my dad who had passed away over six years ago, was there. I bravely responded, "No, Mom. He's not here. Why?" I will never forget what she said next. She said to me, "Because I can see him waiting for me." I immediately ran to Gram and told her what had happened. I think Gram was pretty in and out of it too at that point because she just listened and nodded lightly. I knew what had happened, and it was not one of Mom's hallucinations. The moment was completely different. The way she said it showed some awareness, like she was there again, even if just for a second. It was in the way she spoke. She had also opened her eyes, which she didn't do the day she told me about the pots and pans on her wall or the cat she thought she had seen in her room. It was both a gift and an incredibly depressing moment. It was nonetheless, something I would never forget for as long as I lived.

 In early January of 2011, Tim Jr.'s rec basketball team, "Navy," made it to the playoffs. Tim was eight, almost nine at this point, so he was good but would grow a lot as a player with age. His team made it to the championship at the end of January. His best friend from school and his rec football team played on the opposing team, "Orange." Earl, Delilah, Uncle Colt, Aunt Nat, Gram, and I sat in the blue bleachers and watched from the middle of the court. It was one of those championship games where both teams were equally good and deserving of being there. The entire game consisted of

Tim's team working the ball down the court and scoring. The opposing team would usually answer on their next possession. The game stayed close the whole time, only a few baskets were missed in the hour of play.

In the 4th quarter, it was getting down to the last few seconds. Tim's best friend took the ball with 20 seconds left, passed it to a teammate, and got the ball back from the same teammate a second and a half later. Tim's team was doing a good job defensively. His friend was too good, though, and scored with fourteen seconds left. Tim's coach, with a look of panic, called their last time-out. Uncle Colt turned to Earl, and they had the same look of concern on their face. How would they console Tim in his heartbreak after so much heartbreak? Tim's coach looked at the court, the clock, the court, and the clock until the play resumed. Tim's teammate inbounded the ball to another Navy teammate, who dribbled to mid-court, passing the ball to another teammate, who passed it off to Tim. My heart sank into the pit of my stomach when Tim let the ball fly through the air with one second left. I watched every piece of air this ball touched until the ball soared through the net.

My brother won his basketball championship with a buzzer-beater. We all cried. Tim beamed. I hadn't seen Tim so happy in…a long time. I gave him the biggest hug ever. I felt bad for his friend and the other team, who all cried too. For such a close game and the biggest unexpected shot, it was tough to walk away as the loser. How my little brother calculated that shot so perfectly, I'll never know. He was a good basketball player, but I have full knowledge there was someone else with him that day.

We continued life with as few changes as possible at first. We stayed with Earl at the Ralley house and went to school as he went to his same job. The only difference was Mom not being there, a grand-canyon-sized hole in our hearts that we attempted to leap over each day to find normality. The problem wasn't that we didn't try hard enough. The problem was that our lives, along with all of us, would never be the same. There was no finding of normality. Normality died in 2010, maybe even sooner. No matter how hard we tried, we had to deal with the ways our brains, hearts, and bodies were hurting. It looked different for each one of us, and the only one who had the maturity to do so was Earl. The rest of us were children. We tried desperately to make things work, living in the Ralley house with Earl as Mom had wanted.

One evening, I made my way downstairs to sit with Earl. He had a hockey game on television. I had never actually sat down to watch hockey. As soon as my eyes hit the screen, I was into it. I loved how fast-paced the game was when it seemed my life was excruciatingly slow. I loved how passionate the players were. They hit one another, screamed, and fought. I could tell they felt things in a powerful way. Most of all, I think I loved that this was something to take my mind off the death of my mother. I asked Earl what team this was, and he responded, "This is the local team. You didn't know about them?" I really didn't. That January day in 2011 was when I became a hockey fan. I would lean on hockey a lot to make it.

Later that week, Earl took me, Delilah, and Tim Jr. out to eat. It was late, and we went to the only place in Cherish open 24 hours. I will never forget how the atmosphere was so uneventful. It accentuated our pain. All of us looked at the table. I held back tears, and I remember letting them out once during the meal because I simply couldn't keep them in any longer. Earl looked at me and then the other way. No one knew what to say. It just felt like everything we did highlighted the fact that such a big part of our lives was missing. The worst part was thinking about the cliché saying, "She wouldn't want you to feel like this. She would want you to be happy." While that was true, our pain was valid. And while she wouldn't have wanted it, she would have understood it.

We were exasperated trying to make it work living with Earl at the Ralley house, but we just couldn't. The house was so painful for us. Every room reminded us of Mom. Since Mom had also died there, it felt like everywhere we moved in the home was painted with losing her too. The room I hated going into most was the living room. We had a living room upstairs, but it had no TV. Earl's "man cave" downstairs was our TV room. The upstairs living room with its pink carpet, white couch, and matching white loveseat was there only to look at. We understood this. It was Mom's only-clean-room-in-the-house room. If I zoned out into the distance far enough or closed my eyes, I could picture Mom in her jeans and sneakers, vacuuming the carpet until there were vivid lines. There was a mirror, a small Greek column decoration on which Mom set a plant, and an end table. At the front of the room were the windows with curtains that Mom had set a certain way. They looked beautiful, and we were not supposed to touch them. I don't want you to get the wrong idea, my mom certainly wasn't like this with every room in the house, just this one. She didn't love messes, but she accepted them in every other room of the house. As I've gotten older, I now understand

Mom's need to have one clean room. It brings a level of peace.

Tim Jr. was struggling majorly at school. He was only eight, and his teachers did not know how to help him. He hid under desks and acted out. Earl had to pick him up and meet with the principal on numerous occasions. I was crying myself to sleep and having nightmares. I had nightmares when Mom was dying, and they had returned. I *needed* out, but I didn't *want* out. I wanted to be there. I wanted to stay with Earl. My heart still breaks at the fact that I just couldn't. We just couldn't.

One day, Aunt Natalie and Uncle Colt had us all over. I remember sitting on their stone fireplace while Uncle Colt led the conversation of, "Do you guys want to move in with us?" I knew we needed to. I was so blessed to have an aunt and uncle willing to take us in, but I will never forget the pain in Earl's eyes, who later told me that he never wanted to let go of us kids. He had just lost the woman he loved more than life and was about to lose her children too. Earl was one hell of a dad and person. It was just what we needed to do, and he understood that. It still hurt like hell, though. We moved into Aunt Nat and Uncle Colt's house the next week. They had two sons, who were the same ages as Delilah and Tim Jr. I was the odd one out. Their names were Alexander, who went by Alex, and Jackson. They had to give up their rooms so we could move in. Uncle Colt had to give up his office. It worked out so that the three boys shared a room upstairs. This had originally been Jackson's room. There was a bunk bed in the room, and Aunt Nat put a regular twin bed off to the side. Jackson and Tim took the bunk bed while Alex slept on the bed to the side. I took Alex's old room down the hall. Delilah took Uncle Colt's office in the basement. Her room was tiny because it was never meant to be a bedroom, but she liked it. Earl brought our stuff over in increments. For the first week of living with Aunt Nat and Uncle Colt, Aunt Nat drove us to school. After the first week, we rode the bus because they both worked full-time. Uncle Colt worked for a roofing company as the regional sales manager, and Aunt Nat worked for an OBGYN office in Cherish.

The rest of eighth grade felt like it dragged on forever. I was not okay. I felt like everyone at school kept me at arm's length because they didn't know what to say. That was utterly annoying. I just wanted to be treated like nothing had happened…unless it was a day when the world was caving in. I told Uncle Colt how much I liked hockey and how much it was helping me cope. I had memorized every player on the local professional team along with what number they wore and what position they played. He soon started watching the games with me. It felt so nice to have a hockey buddy. I got Rose into hockey too. I didn't know Mr. Finnley had been a lifelong fan. For a few weeks, I scoured the internet on my little phone to check ticket prices. I found some tickets in the nosebleed section for a reasonable price. I called Earl and asked him, "Would you want to go to a hockey game?" He said he might if the tickets weren't astronomical. I told him they were fairly reasonable. He reminded me that I would have to check with Aunt Natalie and Uncle Colt since I lived with them, and he was no longer the legal guardian. I told him I would, and I did just that at the dinner table. Uncle Colt said he would be happy to go with Earl and I. He suggested we bring along Tim Jr. and that I ask Rose if she wanted to join the fun too. Hearing my uncle not only support something

I desperately needed at the time but encourage it, made my heart light up. The light may have reached out and grasped some of those broken pieces hanging around in my inner being. The game we bought tickets for was later on in the season. I did this because I needed something to look forward to so that I could make it through my eighth-grade year.

When March 30, 2011, finally arrived, we got to leave school early to make it to the game. I don't remember the drive there, but when we got to the arena, Earl and Uncle Colt began to scour the parking garage for a handicapped spot for Rose. Uncle Colt spotted one. Earl had to make a sharp turn, but we managed to secure the spot. We brought signs we had decorated. I hadn't considered the fact that we were sitting too high up. No player would read the sign. It didn't matter, though. I was a heartbroken teenager looking for some peace of mind, and I was just happy to be happy. We had to take the escalators to the top of the arena. It felt like we would never get to our section. When we finally reached the top, we had to find our seats. They were on the other side where the escalator dropped us. We reached them and finally walked through the doorway of our section toward our seats. The players were already out for warm-ups. These were the players I had been watching for the last three months, who had given me hope on my worst days. I couldn't believe they were real. To see their faces as they bounced the puck up the ice and the numbers on the back of their jerseys shone on the arena lights was awe-inspiring.

Our captain was one of the best players in the league. To watch him in his prime gave me the brightest glimmer of hope. I wasn't just watching a good hockey player, who happened to be a professional. I was watching a hockey player who would go down in history as one of the best to ever play the game. The fans cheered his name specifically anytime the puck came his way. I thought about how much pressure that must have been for him. He was tough, and part of why he inspired me was because he always got back up. He rarely got hurt. They said he never broke. He was Rose's favorite player, and he happened to be best friends with my favorite player, the alternate captain. I didn't realize it at the time, but as I looked at these hockey players who knew how to take a hit, I knew I'd be okay if life kept throwing me down onto rock-solid ice. The arena was deafening, and there was something special about that many people cheering on one team together. I felt a sense of community that healed part of my heart that day. Our team ended up losing in a shootout, but it was an enthralling game. I had partly lost my voice, left with a foam finger, and had bought Uncle Colt a shirt. It was one for the books.

 I purchased my first hockey jersey a few weeks later. I found it at a discounted price online, and on the last day of eighth grade, I wore my new, red team jersey down the halls of the school. I had even made a bet with my math teacher that if I passed my standardized test for his class, he'd have to wear my favorite team's t-shirt. I was terrible at math, so he probably figured he wouldn't have to. I'm kidding. I clearly cannot confirm that. I passed, though, and seeing him wear the shirt was the most fulfilling thing I'd experienced in a while. I made him take a photo with me that I still have somewhere. Once the bell rang signaling the last second of eighth grade, Rose and I walked around the school taking pictures of ourselves throughout the building. I ran across the pictures the other day, and I think we did this because we both had endured such a long and dreary middle school experience. Walking out of the school on the last day of eighth grade felt as if we could truly overcome difficulty. I couldn't see how anything would ever be more agonizing than my eighth-grade year.

Aunt Natalie and Uncle Colt's house was in the housing development directly behind Rose's neighborhood. Rose wanted me to meet her at the playground outside of the cul-de-sac near her street the next day. She kept telling me if I walked up my street, there was a connector, and it would drop me right across from the playground. I didn't believe her. I thought the only way to get to her neighborhood was if I walked through Aunt Nat and Uncle Colt's massive neighborhood to the main street and then down the main road to her neighborhood, which was not safe. She called me and assured me of this easier way. She said she had seen it multiple times when Mrs. Finnley dropped me off at my house on the days I rode home from school with Rose.

Rose told me, "Pia. Take the phone with you and just walk up your road. We'll talk while you walk. I'm at the playground."

I responded, "Okay. I'm walking up the street, Rose. I don't think there's a connector. I really don't. Do you know what side of the street it's on?"

"How far are you up your street? I think it's on the left from where you're walking," Rose answered. "You know what? I'll just meet you there. Just walk, turn left at the end of the street, and look for me."

I yelled, "I found you!" Sure enough, there was a connector

street. It had a "Road Closed" sign and was mixed with grass and some pavement. It looked as if it was originally meant to be a full road, but the town decided against it for reasons unknown. I realized I could be in Rose's neighborhood within three minutes of my new house. I was so excited to be able to make it to my old stomping grounds so quickly. Behind Linsell Lane rested Rose's neighborhood, and behind that rested Aunt Nat and Uncle Colt's place. Everything was so connected.

Chapter 11

Simultaneously Weird and Wholesome

In the summer of 2011, Gram took the three of us to visit Mom's cousins and hometown in Massachusetts. There was something special about being in the place my mom grew up so soon after losing her. Life still didn't feel real at this point but getting out of Virginia felt nice for a week. We were surrounded by Aunt Nellie and Uncle Frank, Aunt Cammie and Uncle Ben, and their kids. Aunt Nellie had four children, three girls and one boy. They were Julianna, Brittany, Genevieve, and Nico. Aunt Cammie had three boys: Jeremiah, Matthias, and Jace. One of Mom's other cousins, Tilly, and her husband, made an appearance too. Mom had grown extremely close to Tilly before she passed. I thoroughly enjoyed this trip to Massachusetts as it was so healing to my little hurting heart, but one of my favorite memories of the trip was a Summer Solstice celebration in Aunt Nellie's backyard that she held in memory of Mom.

    Aunt Nellie made posters with pictures of Mom and all of us and hung them up. She made shirts for Gram, Delilah, Tim Jr., and me that had Mom's picture on the front and a picture of our new family with Aunt Natalie, Uncle Colt, Alex, and Jackson on the back. Our last name was Haughman and Aunt Nat and Uncle Colt's was MacPherson, so we called ourselves the MacHaughmans. It was our own kind of legendary family. Aunt Nellie was a salt of the Earth person. She was so close to Mom and reminded me of her in more ways than I could count. She, like Mom, was a mother deep down to her heart and soul. She worked so hard to be there for everyone in her life. I will never forget how happy she was to hand us those T-shirts. I couldn't smile much then, but it meant a whole lot. Aunt Nellie's oldest, Julianna, was a talented equine enthusiast, so she brought her horse to the Summer Solstice and gave riding sessions in the field behind their house. I will never forget watching Julianna go get her horse to bring to the celebration. She rode her horse down the street like it was just another ordinary day, and it reminded me of times long before I existed. We spent the rest of that trip swimming in the Gibson's pool, jumping on the Gibson's trampoline, and visiting Gram's brothers and Mom's old high school. It was all much needed.

    In the weeks and months that followed Mom's death, Aunt Nellie wrote me so many little cards and letters. She did more writing than that. She wrote a letter to Mom's favorite football team and told them all about Mom's deep fandom as well as her situation. One day when Aunt Natalie checked the mail, she found a box addressed to the three of us. I opened it with Delilah and Tim. In it, we found a letter from the head coach of Mom's favorite team stating that he had received a letter from Nellie Gibson. The coach wrote how sorry he was for what we had experienced and said people like Mom were the most valuable part of their team. Inside the rest of the box was a team-signed football, a t-shirt for each of us, water bottles, keychains, and so much more. I was more of a hockey fan those days, but I could appreciate this team's generosity. They could have easily disregarded the letter. Dad and I had watched football together growing up, so I had rooted for Dad's favorite team, the local team, up until this point. Delilah had always rooted for Mom's team, whereas Tim took Dad and I's side. No matter who we rooted for, we each were so appreciative of Mom's team and their wholesome generosity. I was sure no other team would do something so thoughtful.

A few weeks later, in mid-summer, I went on my confirmation retreat. The retreat is a time for the person who is to be confirmed to prepare for their confirmation. It's a time of reflection and prayer. If you are not familiar with what confirmation is, it's a sacrament in the Catholic faith where a person receives the gifts of the Holy Spirit by the placing of oil on the forehead. Through confirmation, the person chooses the faith for themselves. Baptism is the parent choosing the faith for their child; confirmation is kind of the opposite in a sense. It can happen anywhere from grades 8-10, but each diocese is different. Even though I was frustrated with God and would've been okay not getting confirmed, I went for Mom. It meant so much to her that all of us be confirmed. It was something I needed to do despite my feelings toward it at the time. I will never forget the last part of the retreat. A woman announced, "You will now each receive a letter from your parents about this next step in your faith life." I immediately started bawling. Tears were gushing down my face uncontrollably. They started to hand every kid a letter, and I knew I'd be the only one without one. *Why did I have to do this? Maybe I should've disregarded what Mom wanted. This was awful.* That's what was going through my mind at that point. All of a sudden, Mrs. Finnley tapped me on the back and handed me a letter. She gently told me as my tears continued to flow, "As I was writing Rose her letter, I thought about you. I know your mom would have wanted me to do this for you. I hope it reminds you of what she would have said to you today." It was exactly that, everything my mom would have said. The Finnleys deserved a medal.

I attended my high school orientation at the end of summer with Aunt Natalie. It took me back to the same lonely place I was in after Mom died returning to eighth grade. The high school building was massive, and I didn't think I'd ever be able to find my way around. I hated how unknown it all felt to me. I had become extremely displeased by the unknown. Mr. Finnley told me that Rose would have to miss orientation due to a follow-up, so I tried to remember as many details as I could for her. On the first day of high school, I walked through the doors with a boot on my right foot because I had broken my ankle a few days prior while roller skating. I was so frustrated because I was good at roller skating. I just wasn't good at following signs. If I hadn't tried to exit the skating rink through the entrance ramp, it would've never happened. When I did, I crashed right into a man, and my foot went sideways. I tried to walk on it and just knew from the minute I stood up that it was broken. I would have to suffer for a while because of one small decision I made. Of course, I had PE in the first semester. I was so annoyed with myself and my continued streak of bad luck.

I followed Raven to class, not realizing that I had done my usual overthinking again. I walked into the wrong class right when I realized what I was doing. People laughed, but I didn't care. Overall, 9th grade was pretty lonely. I had almost no classes with Raven or Rose and felt like a weird kid with no friends. Kacey from church had gone to the high school her mom taught at in the county over. I was still so introverted that I hung around in the back of the classes, the back of the hallway, yet oddly enough, the front of the bus. I wasn't the best at making new friends, and I ate lunch on the floor outside of the cafeteria because I was too scared to go inside. It was the worst. I remember one day thinking that I should eat in the bathroom, but it was too gross. One day, I went into the cafeteria. I set my things down at a table in the back and got in the lunch line. I'll never forget walking back to the table with my tray in my hands and seeing all my belongings on the floor. A friend group of fellow 9th graders had taken my table and disregarded my things. No one even helped me pick them up. I was so over the annoyance that was 9th grade.

    The rest of the year came and went pretty quickly. My ankle had healed, and I convinced Aunt Natalie and Uncle Colt to sign me up for roller hockey. I loved playing even though there were only two other girls on my first team. I just had to get used to playing a sport I had no experience in and being okay with not being good. I played soccer until I was twelve, and hockey was a lot different. Rose came and watched me play a few games. She was my biggest cheerleader! I wore number nine and loved to see the photos Rose took of me as I played. On the days I had a game, school seemed easier to bear. I was thankful that Aunt Natalie and Uncle Colt were willing to drive me half an hour to and from practices and games. They did so much for us. Later that year, in April, Rose and I were confirmed at Relentless Glory Catholic Church. Aunt Tabitha was my sponsor. My class walked down the aisle in our red robes and received the gifts of the Holy Spirit with our sponsors by our sides. I smiled, took some pictures with Aunt Tabitha, the Bishop, and then took pictures with Rose and Father Theo. We had a gathering at the Ralley house with Earl after the service. Gram had a large cake made that read, "Congratulations, Pia." It felt nice to be on better terms with God.

It was during my 10th-grade year when I met my favorite English teacher, the one teacher who changed everything for me. My days at school became bright, and I looked forward to going. One teacher can make or break a student's experience. Teachers are so powerful; I only wish they all understood this. His name was Mr. Fracassi. There are too many wonderful things about him to recount, but he believed in me, and the light his belief lit inside me is still yet to burn out. He was thin and dressed in a button-down shirt each day. Some days he wore ties but not every day. I could tell he was passionate. Teaching wasn't just an income to him. This was what he wanted to do, craved doing. His classroom was on the first floor, all the way to the end of the hall. It was on the corner right next to the stairwell. He sat me in the middle of the classroom where I had a good view of the whole classroom. He didn't sit much and was very interactive. He liked to move around the room as we engaged with a work of literature. The only times he would sit would be to look out into the room and ask questions, engage with his students, or put his feet up on his desk and place tea bags on his eyelids. I thought it was so strange, but he said teabags can reduce puffiness or redness around the eyes. It turned out that was true. His peculiarity was what kept me paying attention, along with his passion for the work we did each day. He expected us to engage in discourse with him, and he enjoyed hearing what we had to say. He encouraged us to think and share our thoughts aloud.

I'm not sure if he ever knew how much of an outcast I felt or how much I was hurting. I'm pretty sure he found out through the writing we were asked to do each day. He was an advocate for writing…actually writing. Not typing. He said people would forget how to write if they didn't practice often. He also said it was good for our arms. I'm not sure if I have always been a writer, but Mr. Fracassi could tell there was something different in me. I wasn't just his average English student. It was the first time in my life I felt different in a *good* way. This gave me hope for myself. He kept me writing, and he raised his expectations for me. I think I loved English class mostly because of the teacher and mentor Mr. Fracassi happened to be, but I think the course resonated with me because I had lived a life of the few. I knew real pain and suffering at age fifteen. I had the perspective and the maturity of someone many years older. That's why I always felt such a disconnect with people my age. I saw myself in the struggles of the characters, and letting myself analyze them was euphoric in a way. Mr. Fracassi openly encouraged my writing, and it gave me great hope. I'm sure there were many people in my life who believed in me at this point, but Mr. Fracassi's class was where I began to believe in myself again. I felt, after so long in the trenches of grief and loss, that I was capable of possessing confidence and skill in a field. For so long, I neglected to see the light. I found it again in 10th-grade English.

My time living with Aunt Natalie and Uncle Colt was very much like if you were in the dead of winter and spring arrived months early. In a sharp and frigid time, they were pillars of warmth. More than that, they were pillars of strength for me. I have often thought about what it must've felt like for Auntie Nat to have to raise her sister's children after losing her sister, and I can't imagine it would have been easy. I will always be grateful to Aunt Natalie and Uncle Colt for taking us in not knowing the exact difficulties to come but knowing it would be difficult. They did it anyway.

If anyone is reading this and finds themselves in that very situation…living in another family member's household, raising a family member's children, or perhaps some people have been through both, first and foremost, know that you are not alone. I wish I had the answers. There were so many ways in which we would each have to adjust. The process of merging two families was no walk in the park. Even though Mom and Aunt Nat were sisters, our families lived differently. For me personally, I had to get comfortable living in someone else's house until that house truly became my home. Aunt Nat and Uncle Colt's original family would shift in a variety of ways. They all had to be open and understanding of that.

Being accepting of the fact that pretty much everything for all of us was going to change for this to work was key. Uncle Colt suggested that Aunt Nat quit her full-time job to be there for us three kids. We were so fresh in our grief, and we needed someone there with us. To start small, she transitioned from full-time to part-time at her office. Uncle Colt still felt strongly about her quitting her job because their boys also needed her in a greater capacity than she could give while working. She quit shortly after to be a stay-at-home mom and aunt. Going from two to five kids meant many small adjustments along the way. Uncle Colt's parents became another set of grandparents to me, Delilah, and Tim. They had to adjust to having three additional grandchildren who would join them on their summer vacations and holidays. They loved us like their own grandchildren, and it was the cherry on top. Grocery store trips became more expensive, and the back-to-school nights took a lot longer. All of us were new in our grief. We all loved Mom, and due to cancer, we were all making changes. We were making room for grief while the MacPhersons were making room for us…and their grief.

Even though we all knew each other before Mom died, living with extended family was a huge change. I wish I could give families an answer on how to make the process easier. My advice would be to first be open to the changes that need to take place. Don't try to resist them or delay them. My second piece of advice would be to be as gentle as you possibly can with the new family members you are living with. Try to put yourself in their shoes before you judge them, get angry with them, or take something personally. Thirdly, offer an invitation…to ride along to the gas station…to your heart with a silly joke. Know that this is supposed to be difficult. It's okay if you have trouble, and it's okay not to know how to do it all right away. I would add to the second piece of advice to implement that with yourself as well. Be kind to yourself as you navigate this new normal. It's okay to seek advice from the people you love and trust…but trust yourself most of all. Looking back, I feel bad that Aunt Nat probably wanted to ask Mom what to do but couldn't on her hardest days. She could rely on Uncle Colt and Gram, but she had to trust herself to do the best she could for her sister. I would add that she did just that.

About a year into us living with Aunt Nat and Uncle

Colt, Delilah asked to go live with our father's sister, Aunt Jemma. Delilah struggled greatly after the loss of our mom. The saying "Hurt people hurt people," was applicable here. It was brutal for Aunt Nat and Uncle Colt to bear Delilah wanting to leave. In a sense, I think they felt they had failed Mom and the three of us. Delilah, while beautiful as ever, was never good at feeling her feelings. This usually resulted in her running from her pain.

I love my sister, but it didn't make her decision to move away from Tim and me any easier. I wished and prayed on so many occasions that she would realize her strength and be okay. I sometimes wished I could run from my pain too, even for a little. I felt everything so deeply. The more I saw how much she hurt from not knowing her pain, I began to accept the way I always acknowledged mine. The truth was that I couldn't make Delilah stay, and I certainly couldn't change her mind. I could simply be there when she needed me, and that's what I've always tried to do. It was especially hard for me to essentially lose one of my siblings after losing Mom. I wasn't losing her, but it felt like I was. You only get one childhood, and if you can't spend it with your parents, you should at least be able to spend it with your siblings. I knew we would never get this time back. I knew she would likely regret it later on, but there was nothing I could do. I had to let her make her own decisions and deal with the consequences of them. I've never really told anyone just how hard it was for me for Delilah to move away. I thought about my family and when I reflected on the beginning of my life, I just sat in shock at how different things looked now. I knew that no matter what happened, she was ours. She could live with whoever she wanted, but it wouldn't change the facts.

Uncle Colt asked me when Delilah was getting ready to move if Tim and I wanted to go with her. I was downstairs where the walls were lined with Uncle Colt's old soccer jerseys he had hung up as he walked down to find me. I could always hear him coming by the creaks in the steps. He leaned up against the wall. I was on the couch. I turned around, and he found a spot next to me on the couch. He said, "Pia, you know you're always welcome at our house. You are welcome to stay. We hope you do, but we wanted to give you the option to go with Delilah to Aunt Jemma's. We understand if you choose to go, and we won't be offended. Tim is young, so we are asking you to make the decision. We will respect whatever you decide. You don't have to let me know right now." He could tell I was hurting over Delilah leaving. He was too. They had tried to keep her at their house, but it wasn't working. She was too rebellious. Mom called that one. At that moment, I had to decide for both myself and Tim. I thought about how well Tim was finally doing after having such a hard time at school after Mom died. Now, he had a great group of friends. Some of his friends even had families that treated him like a part of their family. I knew how special that was to him. Mom had known these families. His friends' fathers were mentors to him. He was playing football again. I was doing well, too. I had Rose and Raven. I had Mr. Fracassi's class. I was finally starting to see the light. I had grown close to Uncle Colt. I wanted more than anything to be with Delilah, but I couldn't see uprooting my little brother and I all over again. I couldn't see how Delilah wanted that for herself. It was one of the hardest decisions to make. *Mom didn't want us to be separated*, I thought to myself. That was just it. But it wasn't. I knew the adults in my life were all trying their best. It was just a terrible situation. Later that evening, I found Uncle Colt and told him, "I want us to stay." He said, "You've got it." I remember the day Delilah left with Aunt Jemma. Everyone cried. I will never forget that night. I saw Aunt Nat close the door to the front porch. I could hear her weeping. My heart just broke. *This wasn't how it was supposed to be, but was any of it?*

We settled into our new normal as best as we could. I looked at it as a time for me to grow closer to Tim. He had always been closer to Delilah in our younger days, so this was our time. One of Gram's promises to Mom was to drive out to Cherish each Sunday and take us to mass and Sunday school. Mom wanted us all to be confirmed and continue practicing our faith. Gram kept her promise. I felt bad that she had to drive two hours each Sunday, but I remembered that she wanted to, for Mom. She would pick up Delilah on the way out to our house most Sundays. At least on Sundays, we were together again.

I should tell you a little bit about Aunt Nat and Uncle Colt. They both loved with their heart and soul. Aunt Nat and Mom were nine years apart. They were very different. However, the more I got to live with Aunt Nat, the more I saw similarities between her and Mom. I think most sisters are that way. I knew Delilah and I were. Anyway, they were a soccer family. They loved soccer, and Uncle Colt and my cousin Jackson played. They watched soccer on Sundays and practiced soccer tricks in their backyard. Uncle Colt coached Delilah's soccer team when she lived there. They basically breathed soccer. They also liked football and cheered for the worst team ever. I would remind them of this on the regular.

I had introduced them to hockey and created quite the fan out of Uncle Colt. When it came to Aunt Nat, she told it like it was. I was sensitive and fragile at this point in my life, so it took a while for me to get used to her directness. It took a while for her to get used to me too. She hadn't had any daughters. I imagine it was difficult to go from raising only boys to having to raise a girl. She, like Mom, appreciated a clean home and an accurate schedule, and she had a laugh that made everyone in the room want to laugh too.

Uncle Colt was a talented writer and artist, and though he seldom did those things, he was magnificently creative. Uncle Colt was also a backpacker. He would escape into the mountains regularly with only his backpack. I got to accompany Uncle Colt and one of his best friends on a trip into the mountains once. The hike they did was truly "a hike." It was a grueling climb to the top of the mountain but so amazing when you reached the summit. I sat breathless in awe of the fresh air. It hit differently from the top of a mountain. I began to appreciate and come to terms with the difficulties of all my "climbs" while backpacking with Uncle Colt. To add, there was something poetic about carrying everything you'd need for the time you were there on your shoulders and entering into the heart of nature, where all you had was what you carried.

He knew exactly what to do when we stopped for the evening. Backpacking taught me a lot about life. I could see why Uncle Colt enjoyed it so much. It was much like Earl's favorite hobby of fishing. It wasn't relaxing at all, but somehow, it mended the soul. Colt MacPherson did everything he could for his family. He loved Aunt Nat and his boys so much, and he loved us. Once we lived with the MacPhersons, they treated us like we had always been there. My favorite thing about my aunt was how she was continuously present for me. My favorite thing about my uncle was how he always made situations brighter than they were by cracking a joke or coming up with the exact words you needed to hear. After losing Mom, this was such a gift for us.

Chapter 12

The MacHaughmans

One of my favorite things we did as the MacHaughmans was have bonfires in our driveway. Aunt Nat and Uncle Colt lived in a subdivision, so they didn't have as large of a yard as we had in Ralley. Uncle Colt had this small fire pit, and we put it in the driveway with lawn chairs in a circle. Uncle Colt would light the fire, and Aunt Nat would get the materials for smores. As we sat around the fire and bonded with one another, it gave me the heart-warming feeling of being in the presence of family, something I always felt I didn't get enough of. We would share laughs, memories, and smiles, and play games. In one of the games we played, you had to list a famous person, and the next person then had to list a famous person whose name started with the first letter of the previous person's last name. We would go around the little circle until we ran out of names. It was so wholesome, so fun, and pure. At such a young age, I learned to really feel moments of laughter. To take them all in. I had a deep appreciation for laughing so hard your stomach ached. I soaked it in when it happened because it healed me. I saved it in my body for when things weren't so bright.

At one particular driveway bonfire, Uncle Colt realized he had some fireworks left over from the fourth of July. He went to the garage and got the roman candle fireworks out. At this point, it was probably 9:30 to 10:30 at night, but it was a weekend, not a weeknight. Uncle Colt set this roman candle off as we all laughed uncontrollably. He set off two more until the Cherish County cops showed up. I remember saying, "Really?" but when one of them looked at me, I looked the other way. This wasn't the first time the neighbors had called the cops on us MacHaughmans for some good, honest fun. We weren't hurting anybody, and in the grand scheme of things, it wasn't even that loud. It didn't kill our spirit though. Sometimes, Rose would even join our driveway bonfires. I would run up the connecting pathway from my neighborhood to hers. When I found her, I would yell, "We are having a bonfire!" She knew the MacHaughman driveway was the place to be.

The Christmas after Mom died, Aunt Natalie and Uncle Colt did everything they could to make it the best Christmas ever. They knew the one we had the year before. I still say no Christmas beats 2011. I had never had so many presents. It wasn't even the presents that mattered because I've never been materialistic. It was the fact that they put that much thought and effort into making our Christmas great that made me smile. I opened two sets of tickets to see my favorite team play. I had so much fun at the first game; I was so excited to go again. Uncle Colt would take me to one game, and Earl would take me to the other. I loved that I got to go to the games with two hockey fans I loved dearly.

I asked Aunt Nat and Uncle Colt one day if I could paint my room a "basketball orange" color. It was the kind of orange that would require numerous coats if they ever wished to repaint it. I was shocked when they said yes. It took them days to paint it for me. I still remember the orange feeling quirky and different to me. I can't recall why I specifically wanted orange, but it felt like home to me.

Aunt Natalie and Uncle Colt eventually told me they thought I should go to counseling. I had been to counseling after Dad died for a brief time through our church, but I was so young back then, that it was mostly talking and coloring. It would be different now as a high schooler. Uncle Colt had added me and Tim to his health insurance, which was a fantastic policy, so I wouldn't owe anything for my therapy appointments. I wouldn't even have to pay a copay. I trusted Aunt Nat and Uncle Colt's opinion, so I went. My therapist's name was Marley. Even though it was spelled differently than my childhood friend Marly Rye, I still thought it was sweet. I had lost touch with my old friend Marly, but I still thought of her often. Marley's office was right down the road from Aunt Natalie and Uncle Colt's house. I went to counseling once a week for the remainder of high school. I checked myself into school with a note from Marley each week. Marley was an incredible asset in my healing journey. I know everyone feels differently about therapy. It really is personal. I was blessed to be able to go completely covered by my insurance. I am an advocate for it because it has helped me tremendously. With that said, I do believe everyone should find the right therapist for them.

 Uncle Colt worked so hard in every aspect of his life. He drove all over northern and central Virginia making sales as the regional sales manager for his roofing company. He took on us kids and still had to be a father to his boys. He played soccer in the adult league on the weekends. He drove me to hockey games after his soccer games. He laced up my hockey skates and said, "Look, Pia. I don't care if you win this game. I don't care if you score a goal. The only thing I care about is you going out there and skating your ass off.

Do you promise me you'll do that?" He stayed up late with me to work on my English essays. He was a writer at heart, and somehow, when I was beating my head against my notebook trying to find the right words and still lacking them, he found them almost instantaneously. It amazed me how he could just find the words I needed. He also stayed up late with me and worked on math homework.

I remember one night specifically he spent hours on the internet looking at videos and then called one of his friends whose wife taught math, all to help me with fifteen equations. He was the kind of uncle who didn't realize the impact he made. He helped Tim Jr. build his science project. I think the rocket he built with Tim must've taken all weekend. He spent hours helping Alex make the most creative video for a science project on the element beryllium. He took this element off the chart and helped Alex create a true masterpiece, making beryllium seem so empowering and meaningful. He could almost always be found in ripped jeans and a t-shirt. He was funny, creative, selfless, and the way he poured his heart and soul into us kids inspired me. He was the best kind of person.

Uncle Colt spent several weekends building Aunt Nat an outdoor patio. They had lived in their house for a while and always knew they wanted to add to their backyard but could never figure out what to do with it. They couldn't choose between a patio or a deck. Finally, they decided on a patio. Shortly after he built it, we decided to have our first family game night out back to enjoy the summer air, the new patio, and togetherness. It was a lovely evening of happiness. Aunt Nat had to run upstairs for something. When she walked by

Jackson's room, she got the strangest feeling. She opened the door, and that's when family game night changed from carefree to utter chaos. Smithers, our cat, had eaten Jackson's pet bird. He knocked the birdcage off Jackson's dresser, clawed and chewed it open, and all that was left of Jackson's bird was a metal band and the foot it was wrapped around. Feathers covered the floor. Aunt Nat had to sneakily get Uncle Colt from the patio to tell him what had happened. Alex then had to come inside to help Uncle Colt clean up the mess. She then asked Jackson to come see her.

Tim and I didn't know what was happening, but we figured everyone would come back out soon enough. Before long, I heard Jackson scream, "Oh my goodness!" Poor Jackson had just found out what had happened to his bird. Uncle Colt and Alex were upstairs cracking up because they found the only piece left of Mack…his bird foot, while Jackson was having a meltdown. He cried, "Mack must've been so scared, Mom!" Aunt Nat yelled up the stairs to Uncle Colt and Alex, "Be *quiet*! Jackson's really upset." Tim and I stood at the sliding glass door with our eyes wide not knowing what to say. I never did think family game night could be so eventful and disturbing. It was truly one of those moments where we were having such a blissful, peaceful time. It goes to show that you definitely can't plan for something like that. Oh, the chaos of life!

Aunt Nat and Uncle Colt took pictures with me and Rose before my 10th-grade homecoming dance. Mrs. Finnley had dropped Rose off. She wore a purple dress, had her hair curled, and wore black heels. I wore my hair straight, had a pink dress, and wore silver shoes that Gram helped me pick out. We had collectively decided to skip our 9th-grade homecoming, so we had to make an appearance at this one. We were quite a legendary friend pair.

Later that year, Aunt Nat made me get my learner's permit. I say "made me" because had it been up to me, I wouldn't have. Driving seemed scary, and I just didn't want to do it. I didn't pass my learners on the first try due to my overthinking. The frustrating part was I did know it; I just overthought it at the last minute. If you missed one of the signs, they failed you automatically. Thankfully, I passed it on round two. I made sure to keep my overthinking of the signs to a minimum. Aunt Nat and Uncle Colt bought me a cake for passing my learner's test. I forget what it said, but I always thought that was sweet. They both taught me how to drive. I do think I made Aunt Nat a nervous wreck because I veered too much to the right.

Uncle Colt did most of the driving instructions one-on-one. He drove over to the high school parking lot, not my high school, but the other one in town. He showed me how to back into a spot several times and then had me try it. Each time, he would reiterate the steps and communicate how I had parked in relation to where I should have been. He would grab the wheel if needed to show me exactly which way I needed to turn. If I had kept up practicing, I would probably be a pro at backing into spots today. Unfortunately, it was still scary after he showed me, so I didn't try to back into parking spots on my own. I do, however, remember so many of his driving tips. One in particular makes me laugh anytime I think about it. I was a little overly cautious about this whole driving thing. We were on one of the main roads in town. I must've been exhibiting some sort of nervousness about driving when he said, "Your eyes should always be out in front of you. Not behind you. I know you are scared of what other people are doing but listen, Pia. The *last* thing any driver wants to do is hit another car."

He then grabbed the wheel and purposely pushed my vehicle over the double yellow lines. I was severely confused. I gave him a look as if to ask if we needed to drive over to the hospital. He just told me the last thing any driver wanted to do was hit another car, yet here he was driving over the line purposefully. You must not forget that Uncle Colt always knew what he was doing. He continued, "See. Even if you are over the line, they'll move." He pointed at a passing car, and the driver glared at us as they passed. Uncle Colt continued, "You will get a lot of strange looks, but they'll move." This gave me confidence. I knew at that moment that even if I were to veer too much to the right or too much to the left, I'd be okay.

One day, Uncle Dallas reached out to Aunt Natalie and said he wanted to get me a car. I was so grateful because this was so incredibly nice, and I missed Uncle Dallas a lot. Although, I wondered if I'd even be able to have a car because I didn't even have my license yet. Aunt Nat told Uncle Dallas that I had just gotten my permit...and that we didn't have anywhere to store the car until I got my license. He bought it for me anyway and sent it to our house. It was a car from the year I was born, but he put a lot of work into fixing it up for me. Uncle Dallas was a big shot in the car industry and had worked his way there from pumping gas. It was pretty impressive. I always admired that about my uncle. The car was purple, and I had so many plans for where I would take it one day. It would have to be parked on the street across from our house until I got my license since there was no room in the driveway or garage.

Unfortunately, one of our neighbors up the street decided to throw a party one evening. Someone at that party tried to drive home drunk. This person ended up smashing into my car. Their car flipped, and they slid a good distance up the street. It woke everyone up: the jerk neighbors who called the cops on us, Aunt Nat and Uncle Colt, Tim, Alex, and Jackson. The person somehow got out of their car after sliding up the street and attempted to run away.

Someone called the police (probably our neighbors) and they arrested the person. I was quite the deep sleeper in my high school days. I slept through the entire night. I have no idea how that was possible because according to everyone in the MacHaughman household, it sounded like a freight train hit our house at two in the morning.

When I got up the next morning, I could tell that everyone was looking at me rather oddly. I walked into the kitchen to make some coffee when Uncle Colt looked at me and whispered, "Need to talk to ya, lady." I just knew it was bad. I was thinking someone died...but it was *something* that had died. He then said, "Your car was hit by a drunk driver last night." I wasn't even awake. I think I asked him something like how that was even possible because it was just sitting there. He said, "Come on. I'll show you." I walked out to my smashed-up car holding a bagel at 11 am. It felt like I really couldn't have anything in life. It would all be snatched from me. The insurance company ended up coming out to the house later that week and writing Aunt Nat and Uncle Colt a check for what it was worth. It was worth a little over $3,000. I didn't have my license yet, so I wasn't in a huge rush to go car shopping. I wanted to wait as long as we could, honestly. I felt so agonized by the whole thing. I didn't even care to look for a car until I had my license in hand. Uncle Colt waited a few months and then said we would go look at this used car place after school. I was unenthused but complied. I remember us walking around the lot seeing if anything caught my eye. I did peer into a few of the windows and tried to picture myself driving them, but nothing stood out.

 Uncle Colt finally pointed out this white car toward the side that had missed my view and said, "What about that one?" *It wasn't bad,* I thought to myself, and it was in my price range. We went and got the owner to tell him we were interested in purchasing it. Uncle Colt asked the man, "Is there any chance you can go $500 lower?" The guy was wincing as he didn't want to lower the price but wanted to make the sale. He said, "I don't think I can." Uncle Colt said, "Are you sure you can't go even $400 lower?" The man said okay, still wincing. He ran inside to run the paperwork and the check. When we made it back to Uncle Colt's car, he said he wanted to do that so that I would have some money left over for insurance and gas. I'm not sure who broke the news to Uncle Dallas about the car, but someone did. I don't remember his reaction, but I always felt bad that it had happened. No matter how distant Uncle Dallas was or would become, I will always remember and be thankful for this nice gesture. I didn't know why the universe felt the need to keep smacking me around. Thankfully, I had people like Aunt Nat and Uncle Colt to smack it right back for me.

On another note, Aunt Nat and Uncle Colt knew I had social media and posted regularly about random things, mostly hockey and high school. They were friends with me and followed all that I posted online. I didn't tell them that I had met a friend a few years older than me named Brady and messaged him about our favorite hockey team sometimes. I don't know why I hid that information from them. I guess at this point, social media was still pretty new, and people were somewhat skeptical. My mom had also told me not to talk to strangers. I heard her voice in my head when I thought about the fact that I disregarded a piece of her advice. I thought Aunt Nat and Uncle Colt would freak out or tell me to stop talking to him since he was a stranger paired with the fact that I was fifteen and he was nineteen. I would've probably done that if I were in their shoes and my niece told me she had talked to a stranger online.

We were just friends, and I didn't see anything wrong with having a virtual friend. It was just like every other friend I had in my life, only he had never met me in person. It's not like he knew where I lived or anything. He randomly popped up on my feed one day, and I followed him. He followed me back. I don't remember how, but we became friends after I posted something that resonated with him, and we talked now and then. He lived in Virginia too but a few hours from Cherish. He was the kindest soul and a good friend during those years. How he popped up on my feed, I'll never know. We had zero mutual friends. It was the biggest blessing from the social media world. He said he felt horrible about all the things I had to go through. I didn't know at the time how much Brady cared about me, or the ways he would go on to impact my life. I could tell that he was a genuine person who cared about someone he had never even met. It felt nice to have a friend that knew me from afar. It felt like everyone thought they knew me because they knew what I had been through. The truth was very few people knew me at that time. I knew my aunt and uncle would've liked him, but it wasn't the time to tell them about my virtual friend.

One day after school, Alex, Jackson, Tim, and I went into the pool parking lot in our neighborhood to play some street hockey. Alex had recently decided to start playing and was on my roller hockey team this year. We grabbed the extra sticks in the garage and I grabbed some cones to use as "nets". During a face-off, Tim picked up his hockey stick in a swift motion, and I felt it hit my face. What felt like a small scratch had ripped two small lines open across my face, indents from the older stick he was using. I felt a small amount of blood come to the surface. I finished the game and cleaned myself up as best as I could once we got home. It did not look good… It turns out that same day, Jedediah Finnley sprained his wrist and bruised a part of his arm. Rose asked me if I wanted to go out to eat at the twenty-four-hour diner in Cherish to cheer him up. I confessed to her that while I wanted to go, I hadn't found a way to cover my gnarly facial cut. Rose assured me not to worry, and I met her there. The hostess sat Jedediah, Rose, and me at a booth in the back. I glanced at the menu, even though I knew what I was going to order. I got the same thing every time I ate here. However, sometimes I would switch it up and get pancakes. I was going to start with their seasonal, festive latte. The waiter danced his way from the kitchen to our table. He was mouthing the words to whatever was playing on the radio as he shuffled along the tile floor to us. He stopped in his tracks as he reached us and with both eyebrows raised said, "You guys look beat up." I was confused at first, but as I looked across the table at Rose with her loft strands, Jed with his sling, and me with a lovely scrape across the entire left side of my face…it made sense. We were a little messed up, but we wouldn't let that stop us.

When I think of how best to sum up my time as a MacHaughman, I'm not sure there are words of enough quality to describe how I feel about those years. There were too many wonderful memories to recall. The majority of them I will leave in our hearts. During the MacHaughman years, I was hurting and trying to piece myself together. I was wondering about the rest of my life. In those years, I knew I had something special, but I didn't know what a gift those years truly were. As I sit here now 12 to 13 years later, I know those years will stand strong as some of the best. They gave me joy no one will ever be able to take away from me. They gave me a sense of community. They gave me love only family can give, and we were a top-notch family, if I do say so myself.

Uncle Colt was also an avid athlete. If he wasn't on the soccer field or backpacking away from society, he could be found in the gym lifting weights or jogging. He had surgery a few years ago to help his bum knee, and he continued to play soccer, staying active despite his metal knee or doctor's predictions. He was jogging in the main park in the middle of the town of Cherish when he witnessed two men fighting. As he was rounding the corner, one of the men flashed a gun and shot the other man. Uncle Colt yelled, "Hey!" and approached the man who had been shot. Realizing it was serious, Uncle Colt ripped off the shirt he was wearing and applied pressure to the injured man's wound. Once the shirt was secured around the man's arm, Uncle Colt called the Cherish County police. The man who had chosen violence was no longer in sight. Later, Uncle Colt was summoned to court as a witness in the case. The judge at one point asked Uncle Colt to stand up. She continued, "Sir, at any point, did you witness either of these men exhibiting any aggressive behaviors?" Uncle Colt answered, "Yes, your honor." He pointed at the shooter and continued, "When that man shot the other man, I'd say that was pretty aggressive." As he told us this while he smoked brisket one evening, I thought about how much Cherish had grown and changed since first arriving with my beautiful parents. That park used to be so nice and safe. My mom had taken me there to play when I was a kid, and Mrs. Reese had gone on a walk with me there after my dad died. I had this distinct awareness that I did not like my hometown becoming tainted in any way. I wanted to keep it as pure as it was in my memory.

Chapter 13

Paper Mache, Gas, and a Triple Cheeseburger?

The Finnleys ran Vacation Bible School at Relentless Glory Catholic Church. Rose asked me to help each year, and I had so much fun doing it. Mr. and Mrs. Finnley spent multiple days, the entire day, setting up before the start date. This year was a campfire theme. Mr. Finnley built a paper mache fire, and we made tents to set around the parish hall. Rose told me that she would find a station for me to work with her. There would be five stations: a food station, a craft station, a story station, a singing and dancing station, and an outdoor station. We got to help with the singing and dancing station. There was a video for the children to watch, and Rose and I would do our best to act out the moves the people in the video were showing. This was paired with singing a song about the Bible. Each day of VBS, the kids had a new song and dance to learn. Rose was a natural at working with children…and singing.

    I eventually had to go help with the food station because they got a little overwhelmed. It was such a lovely experience overall for the kids of our church. I had to go to the bathroom at one point, and right as I was reaching for a paper towel, I heard Mr. Finnley scream, "NOOOOO!" at the top of his lungs. I tried to get back out to the parish hall as fast as possible in case something terrible had happened. When I walked through the double doors, I saw a kid stomping on his paper mache fire, destroying the creation he had spent days making. The kid must've gotten away from their group. I looked over at Rose, who seemed terrified. It wasn't funny, but looking at Rose made me want to laugh, and then I could see the need to laugh within her as she looked at me. We really shouldn't have been allowed to glance at each other in serious situations.

I returned home to a MacHaughman house after VBS where no one would be laughing. Tim and Jackson had decided to sneakily egg several of our neighbors' houses for no reason, who had all confronted Uncle Colt about the situation. He was pissed. He made Tim and Jackson apologize to every single person. They also had to clean the doors of each neighbor they egged. The angriest neighbor didn't even live in their house. They were set to rent it out and when the renters arrived to move in, they were met with eggs stuck to the door. The heat had made the eggs runny and exude a disgusting odor. That door took them the longest to clean. It had to look immaculate for them to avoid being grounded. On another note, Alex was attempting to walk downstairs but tripped. He slid down three stairs, and his leg went through the wall. After dealing with Tim and Jackson, Uncle Colt told Alex, "Get down here, *now*! Today is the day you learn to fix drywall." Again, none of this was funny, but I felt like laughing. I took that as a good sign.

As I looked at the chaos around me, I thought about how I had finally gotten my license. Rose wasn't able to get hers at the same time as me even though she was a month older. Due to her hip surgery that made her need to use the loft strands, she would need to drive with her left foot and not her right, or she would need an extension on her pedal for her right foot to reach the gas. Mr. Finnley was working with her doctors to get this achieved eventually, but it would take some time. For the time being, I would have to drive to Rose or pick her up. I remember the first day of driving successfully. Aunt Natalie and Uncle Colt were so proud. I began to pick Tim up from football practices to help Aunt Nat and Uncle Colt out and did little things for Aunt Nat when she asked, but the best part was driving myself to school. I did not like to ride the bus. There was this one thing about my car…the gas gauge did not work. It was a '96, not the most tech-savvy car in 2013. I had to guesstimate how much gas was in the car by remembering when I filled it and how much I drove each time. It was pretty exhausting. I was supposed to be picking Tim up from football practice one evening when I turned the corner onto Cavern Road. As I finished the turn, I felt my wheel lock. I was unable to move the wheel to the left and my car just stopped, right next to Dr. Wales's office. I called Uncle Colt thinking something was wrong with my car. He showed up with Aunt Natalie and Alex, who were prepared to call a tow truck. After checking my car out, Uncle Colt side-eyed me pretty hard. I looked at Aunt Natalie, who looked at Uncle Colt, and then to Alex.

"I'm going to go pick up Tim," uttered Uncle Colt. "She's out of gas."

I responded, "Oh my gosh." Panic filled me. It had been such a long day at school. I just wanted to pick up Tim. I had stayed up until 2 am doing history homework the night before. I knew I was overly tired. I continued, "I'm sorry. I would have just figured it out myself without calling you if I knew that's what it was. I just put gas in it earlier this week." I paused, placing my hand on my forehead, realizing I hadn't filled my car up in over a week. "Ugh. It wasn't earlier this week. It was last week, and I didn't completely fill it."

"It's okay," reassured Uncle Colt. "You will just have to make sure you keep a really good eye on it. We can tape an index card to your dash, so you always know the last time you filled up." I hated that I had inconvenienced everyone for the evening. The whole point of my driving to get Tim was to help, not make life more difficult. Aunt Natalie had been working on dinner, too.

"Well, Alex and I will go to the gas station and get some gas," Aunt Natalie offered.

"You're going to have to buy gas containers too. The ones I had in my car are no longer in there," said Uncle Colt. I was still inconveniencing everyone. I felt awful. I was also costing them money. I then thought about how this had happened in a pretty good spot if I was ever going to run out of gas. Right next to Cavern Road was a gas station. Aunt Natalie and Alex brought me gas, and I was sure I'd never allow that to happen again.

I got to see Rose more often having my license. I still asked Aunt Nat and Uncle Colt for permission to go places, but Rose would call me often with ideas for adventure. Sometimes Raven would hang out too, and I would drive to see Raven and Penny regularly. Rose asked me one day if I wanted to drive her and Jed to her grandparents' house. Her parents would drive her siblings, but this way they could take one car instead of two. Mr. and Mrs. Finnley, her grandparents, were just as special to me as Mr. and Mrs. Finnley, her parents. The only issue was that Rose would rarely tell them when I was joining her and coming along for the visit. My mom had implanted in me the sense that it was wrong to show up without asking if it was okay first. I asked Rose on the drive there if she had told them this time, and she said her usual, "They won't care. You're like family." I responded, "I know! I just wish you would tell them." A second of silence met us and I continued, "Did your parents tell them?"

"I don't think so. It's fine, Pia!" Rose assured me. I sighed. When we got to her grandparents' house, they opened the door and said, "Pia! All are welcome!" We spent the day swimming and lounging in the hot tub with Rayne, Jedediah, Jimmy, and Rose's cousins. As we swam, I looked at Rose in the pool and asked her, "Do you remember that time my mom and I went to see Josh in his last school musical performance and your grandparents were there with you all?" Rose nodded. I kept going, "Remember when I saw you guys and told Mom we had to sit next to you? When we reached your aisle, your grandma whipped a cheeseburger out of her purse and said so nonchalantly to my mom, 'Triple cheeseburger?'" Rose squirted water out of her mouth she was laughing so hard.

"It was hilarious," I snorted. "My mom didn't know what to say!"

Mr. Finnley later talked about how he found Rose a silver car for a reasonable price. It was several years newer than my car, and he was going to try to purchase it for her. Her eyes beamed, and she reminded him she wanted her license plate to say "ROSEYY."

Chapter 14

The Moments We'll Remember

The time came for Tim and I to move back to the Ralley house and live with Earl. The best way I can describe it was that it was time. We all knew it. As we were getting ready to move back, Uncle Colt said to me, "I kind of figured you guys would circle back there one day." I looked over at him and asked, "You did?" He responded, "Yeah. It's your home." I drove out to Ralley one afternoon before we moved back. I felt my phone vibrating and looked down to see Aunt Jemma was calling me. I answered, and she asked me if it was true that Tim and I were going to move back to our mom's house and live with Earl. I told her it was. She asked me, "Are you sure?" I said, "Yes. I think this is the right move for us, no pun intended." She said, "Okay, honey."

We moved back to Ralley with two and a half months left of my junior year of high school. Delilah's old room had become Earl's office, so Tim and I moved our things into our old rooms. Our belongings fit perfectly as if they had never been moved to begin with. It felt…nostalgic. I asked Earl if we could paint my room white to signify a fresh start in my life. He agreed, and we spent a few days painting. It took several coats to cover the turquoise paint that 11-year-old Pia had requested. When Earl said it was dry and I could go take a look, the white paint had a blue tint to it. I thought it was a little symbolic. It was as if Mom was saying *I'm still here. I never left.*

Earl had done everything he could to keep the Ralley

house while we took our detour to live with Aunt Nat and Uncle Colt. He had bought the house with Mom on two incomes, so it took some changes for him to keep it on one. He closed the doors to keep the heat in during the winter, canceled the cable, and so much more. I asked him one day why he stayed here, why he bothered to keep the house. His response, "I wanted to in case you guys ever needed to move back here," made me realize that if all men were a little bit more like Earl Rhoades, the world would be a better place. The fact that he stuck around for us kids years after losing Mom amazed me. It would have been easy for him to sell the house, move on, and leave us behind. He didn't.

He was the only father Tim remembered. He gave me the chance to experience longer than seven years of a father's love. I was so grateful my mom had found a man like him.

The time came for Tim Jr. to be confirmed. Tim mentioned to Gram that he didn't know what saint to pick for his confirmation saint or who to ask to be his sponsor. He decided on St. Thomas Aquinas, but he still hadn't chosen a sponsor. Gram told him, "I think you should ask Pia." One day, Tim handed me a small box tied together with a red ribbon. The box must've been from a pair of earrings I got one Christmas. The name on the front was Mom's name. *Catalina Jewelry Co* was printed across the box in cursive. When I opened it, there was a small note that read, "Will you be my sponsor? Love, Tim" Of course, I said I'd be honored.

The rest of my junior year wasn't super interesting, but Rose got her license! I told her I was going to make her drive me around everywhere now. She told me she'd be happy to do just that! She picked me up in Ralley one Sunday evening, and we drove around through Ralley's windy roads with the windows down feeling fearless. When Rose went to merge onto the main highway, another car had been speedily rounding the corner. It was a tricky spot because even though you could see, cars drove around that corner so fast. Rose had had enough time, but the other driver switched lanes and gestured an annoyed look at Rose. I told her about the look of disproval on the other lady's face, and Rose blew it off. I was so proud of my friend for overcoming her cancer and its aftereffects. She drove down that highway and you'd never have known the rain she had previously trudged through. The blue sky was too overwhelming, and her hair was in her face. I thought to myself, *show me a better duo than us two.*

Senior year eventually arrived. I never thought about my senior year much due to the many other things that crowded my mind. When it finally graced me with its presence, Earl hugged me in the kitchen where Mom used to bake. Behind us hung the wallpaper my mom had started to remove but didn't quite complete removing. I always thought the patch left there was meaningful to the eye. I had managed to get a parking spot right by the door, so I didn't have a long walk once I got to the school. It was a nice-sized student lot, so I was grateful, especially since it looked like it was about to drizzle. I walked through the doors of my high school on the first day of senior year to find Rose and Raven waiting for me. I met them with an unapologetic smile, and we were off to class.

Rose and I went to homecoming a few months later. We got ready in Ralley at my house, and we picked up Jedediah on the way to school for the dance. On the way to my house,

Rose's left side-view mirror had cracked and was falling slightly off her vehicle, so Earl taped it on and said it would be fine. She was so nervous, but Earl was right. We danced the night away. Raven found us in the crowd. She looked simply stunning. For a moment, everyone around me became fuzzy, and we were the only ones in the room.

At the next home football game a few weeks after homecoming, I met Rose at the entrance gate. She had a strange look on her face. I had anxiety, and it made me feel uneasy. I asked Rose, "Tell me. What is wrong?"

Rose replied, "Nothing is wrong, Pia. Swear." I looked at her to send a message that I knew she had something to say. She continued, "I have a question for you, and I hope you say yes."

I told her, "I'm sure I will, Rose. What is it?" Rose waited a brief second until we had reached the other end of the football field by the end zone and said to me, "I want you to write my eulogy and read it at my funeral one day." I stopped dead in my tracks. I could hear cheering in the background, but my world stood still. I assured Rose, "You are not dying, Rose." She said, "I know. It would just mean a lot to me if you would say yes." I proceeded with a look of question but answered, "Yes. I'll do it." She smiled, nodded, and thanked me.

I was introduced to a girl by the name of Aria a couple of days later. Rose and Aria had met in science class when they were assigned to be partners on a project. They became friends while working together, and Rose told me she thought highly of her. Aria had a wonderful spirit, and I knew we would get along well too. Rose had to wait for Jedediah to make his way down to the parking lot. She suggested to Aria and me, "We should get a bite to eat down the road." I didn't have anything to do besides history homework, so I agreed, as did Aria, and we met each other there. We all sat together at a booth near the front. Rose hadn't finished her meal and said she would save the rest for later. There were three chicken nuggets left. Jedediah asked, "Can I have one?" pointing to her box. Rose replied, "You can have *one*."

Rose and I conversed with Aria. I was enjoying getting to know her, and I could tell it made Rose happy we were getting along. Rose looked over to her brother, who had eaten the remainder of her chicken nuggets. Rose snapped, "I told you that you could have one! Not the rest of them!" Jedediah looked confused. He explained, "I'm sorry. I was hungry!" Rose scowled, to which Jed continued, "I didn't think you wanted them." Rose was pissed. I looked at Aria. Jedediah and Rose knew how to butt heads. I hoped it wasn't going to be a blow-up.

Rose got up, declared, "Well, I'm leaving!" and left. Aria and I grabbed our things. "Rose!" I yelled, but she kept walking, got in her car, and drove off. I was standing in the parking lot holding my half-empty milkshake wondering what to do. Jedediah met us outside. I just looked at him with a blank stare. Rose had driven him there, and she was supposed to be his ride home.

"I...I guess I can take you home. Unless Rose is just kidding, and she plans to come back" I said to Aria and Jed. Aria chimed in, "How about I wait with Jed for a few to see if she comes back? If not, I live closer to the Finnleys than you do, Pia. I will just drive him back home." At the same moment Aria's sentence finished, Rose pulled back into the parking lot. Rose loved chicken nuggets, but she loved her brother more.

The Fault in our Stars by John Green was released in June of 2014, and it hit home for Rose. It was a book about a girl and a boy who both had cancer, met at a support group, and fell in love. The book became a movie too, and the movie became available at the Cherish movie theatre months later. It wasn't often something so personal to Rose was portrayed in the media. She told me all about the book and wanted me to read it. She said, "How about we watch the movie, and if you like that, then you can read the book?" I agreed. Rose talked to Raven, and we decided to meet at Raven's house after school one afternoon to watch it. The movie ended up crushing my soul, and I stormed out in the middle of the movie to my car and drove away. Rose and Raven stood on Raven's porch and watched me drive away. They tried calling me a million times, but I let them all go to voicemail. The movie brought back a rush of emotions from when my mom had been sick. It also gave me the fear of what it would be like to lose Rose.

Rose asked me the next day at school if I was okay. I told her I was and apologized for leaving the way I did. I told her I'd even apologize to Raven too. Rose said they weren't mad at me; they were just worried. I told Rose that it had been so hard for me to watch my mother and best friend fight the same illness. I hated watching them both suffer through cancer's wickedness. She nodded and said, "Well, you can finish the movie if you want, but you don't have to…I understand either way." I continued, "Rose, I know how much it means to you for me to watch the movie. The *full* movie. So, I'm going to finish it." I finished the movie two days later with a box of tissues in my lap, tears streaming down my face.

"I hate that I'm such a wimp," I sniffled.

"Pia," Rose said. She looked at Raven who was sitting on the other side of the room and continued. "We both think you've been a little too strong." I wiped another tear away.

That Halloween, Rose said she wanted me to dress up as the guy character from the movie, and she was going to dress up like the girl. No one in our youth group would expect us to show up as a costume pair. I jokingly asked Rose, "Are you asking me to be your man?" Jedediah had spread a rumor once when he was mad at Rose that we were lovers and not friends, so it seemed fitting. Rose said she could use some medical tubes she had sitting in her room from when she got her PICC line to make an oxygen tank. It would take some piecing together for me to truly become Rose's man. I spent time in our kitchen looking for a pretzel I could use as a fake cigarette until I thought of something better. A straw.

I cut the straw in half and placed it between my fingers. It was perfect! I then went into Tim's room and opened his closet looking for a shirt, sweater, or jacket that felt fitting for my character. I ran into some of our father's old clothing Tim had hanging up. I came up empty. Nothing felt right. I did snatch a pair of Tim's sneakers to wear. I remembered I had a tan leather jacket in my closet. I went to grab it to remind myself if it would be right for the costume, and it was! I put my hair in a low ponytail and then put my ponytail in the back of my shirt. I was the perfect male character, and from now on I would always refer to myself as Rose's incredibly attractive male friend.

Later that semester, my physics teacher gave us an assignment. The directions were to design a car that could move a small distance. It had to be able to move a yard or two. We could use whatever materials we wanted. I was truly lost. I could write a paper so phenomenal that Mr. Fracassi called me Dr. Haughman, but I could not make a car. Even one made out of popsicle sticks. I confided in Rose about how stressed this project was making me. She told me that she could make me a car; she was sure of it. Rose didn't take physics because she was going for the standard diploma and didn't need it. She wanted the advanced diploma more than anything, but with the number of days she had to miss for follow-ups and precautionary treatment, it would have been extremely difficult. Mr. and Mrs. Finnley, along with her counselor, convinced Rose to go for the standard. They said it was just as big of an accomplishment as the advanced. She didn't want to give up the advanced diploma dream, but she did. I felt like she should have been the one out of the two of us to pass physics. I told her if she could make me this car I'd pencil her name in on my advanced diploma. She laughed and told me to meet her at the craft store the next morning. As we walked through the aisles, Rose told me all about her intricate design plan and explained why she was buying each particular piece. I stood there dumbfounded but shaking my head like I knew what she was saying. Rose was amazingly creative. We planned to set it up at my house. As we got to the parking lot, I quizzed Rose. "Does my tire look flat to you? It felt weird driving into town." Rose gave me a stare as I gave her when she was explaining the craft materials for the car. "I don't know!" she said.

"Well, will you go with me to put air in my tire? I don't want to go alone, and I'm not sure how to do that," I told Rose.

She responded, "Yeah, of course I will." She hopped in my passenger seat. I pulled into the gas station parking lot and parked close to the air machine. Rose got out and walked over to the machine, saying, "It's 75 cents!" I looked in my cupholders and said, "Here. Would you mind starting it? I'm going to get the cap off my tire." Rose handed me the pump after she put the quarters in. The machine was ridiculously loud. I could tell my eardrums would be aching after standing close to this machine.

"It's on, right?" I asked Rose.

Rose tilted her head and said, "It looks like it is?" I was bending over staring at the pump on my tire. Rose began to crack up. I looked at her and began to laugh too. People were driving by, watching two 18-year-old girls make fools of themselves.

I said, "Seriously, Rose! It's going to time out, and I'm scared to drive home on a tire with low air." We were practically screaming at each other because the machine was so loud.

Rose offered, "Let me try!" I moved out of her way. I gave it a few seconds and then jumped in, "Okay! Stop! Take it off! I don't want my tire to explode. How do I know if it's too full? I don't have one of those tire pressure things that Earl keeps in the garage." Rose just looked at me. I then began walking around my car, observing the three other tires, and comparing it to the one I thought was flat. I told Rose, "Okay. Now this tire looks too big!" Rose was doubled over laughing hysterically. The machine was still roaring behind us. I put the cap back on and drove Rose back to the craft store to get her car.

Rose turned eighteen on November 13, 2014. She called me the following week and said she wanted to go to the gas station to get a slushie drink. I looked at my phone. It read 11:32 pm. I said, "Rose…you do remember you have your license, right? And you're a lot closer to the gas station than me." Where I lived in Ralley was in the county of Cherish about fifteen minutes away from the town of Cherish where Rose's house was. She told me, "Pia! Come on. This could be the first wild thing we do now that I'm eighteen." I rebutted, "Well, I'm not eighteen!" She countered, "Yeah, I said now that *I* am eighteen." Rose Finnley was serious, and she wasn't about to let me get out of this adventure.

"Do you want me to come get you? Is that what you're asking?" I questioned.

"*Yes*," Rose said.

"You can't just drive yourself, huh?" I remarked.

"Pia. We have been friends for forever. You know if I'm going to do something crazy, you are going down with me. I would drive us, but I'm afraid my mom would hear my car start and stop me, and I really want a slushie."

I inhaled. Just as I was about to speak, Rose said, "And Jedediah wants to come too. He wants a snack."

"Fine!" I said. "I'll go. I'll be there in fifteen." I could hear Earl snoring from my room, and Tim was still up playing video games.

"Yes!" Rose shouted. "I gotta be quiet, but that's the Pia Haughman I know and love." I laughed.

I arrived and made a U-turn in the famous cul de sac behind Linsell Lane, arriving at the Finnley's house a few minutes before midnight. I sent Rose a message letting her know. She and Jed snuck out the front door a few minutes later. When they got buckled, I asked, "Are you guys sure your mom isn't going to get mad at me for this? I really would prefer it if she liked me."

Rose said, "Pia, if she does, she will be mad at me and not you." It was past midnight when I pulled up to the gas station. I got my slushie and told Rose and Jed that I'd be out in the car waiting on them. I was so scared of getting Rose in trouble. Jed exited the gas station first with his snack, and Rose followed with her slushie. Right as I shifted my car into reverse, Rose's phone rang.

"Crap!" Rose announced. "It's Mom."

"Just let it ring," suggested Jedediah.

"Oh gosh!" I exclaimed.

Rose let it ring a few times, then answered.

"Rose Eliana Finnley," uttered Mrs. Finnley in the sternest voice I had ever heard her use.

"Where are you?"

"Mom, we just went to the gas station to get slushies. Pia drove. "We are pulling into the neighborhood now," Rose lied. My hand smacked my face in disapproval. We were at least five minutes from their neighborhood.

"Rose Finnley!" Mrs. Finnley continued. "You are eighteen, not twenty-one years old! You cannot just leave the house at midnight without telling me. You've got your little brother in the car too!"

I hoped I'd be welcomed at the Finnleys in the future.

It was December, and I was on the phone with Delilah trying to decide on Christmas gifts for the family when I saw Rose's car pull into my driveway. It was rare for Rose to show up unannounced. I told Delilah, "I have to go," and hung up without thinking twice. I grabbed my sneakers and ran to the door as fast as I could. My hands were shaky. I opened our red front door as Rose got out of our car. When I opened the screen door and saw her, she didn't look good. I could tell she had been crying. My face offered a concerned look. I approached Rose, and she sniffled as she said, "They found cancer in my lungs on my scan today. It's also around my spine. It's back." She cried, "I can't believe it's back." As I hugged my best friend, I gazed at the sky from the same spot in my yard, just as I did on the December day Mom passed away.

Chapter 15
Blue Skies

A few months later, on March 25th, I got a call from Jedediah saying the cancer had spread to the sac around Rose's heart. I had just finished up a fundraiser for our school's cancer research fundraising club. It wasn't the same without Rose. I heard what Jed said, but I didn't know what I was doing. It felt like my body was moving and I was just standing there watching it. I met them at the Cherish hospital that evening where her grandparents, parents, and siblings were. They were all crying. Oh, the feeling. It re-visited me that day. *This couldn't be it. Rose and I had so much more to do.*

    The next day, I went over to the Finnleys, sat on the edge of Rose's bed, and held her hand. My eyelids were the size of overgrown grapes. Hospice had been called. The following day, on March 27th, it was Tim's 13th birthday, and for some strange reason, I went to school. I shouldn't have, but I had this odd desire to power through and be strong every day of my life. I was getting tired of being strong. I didn't want to be strong. I didn't want strength. I wanted softness. I wanted peace. My eyes felt like they were dragging my entire body down. I was so glad senior year gave me the gift of having my favorite English teacher for the second time. Yet, that day when it came time to go to Mr. Fracassi's class, I didn't even feel good about going. English class gave me the same feeling as every other class did that dreary day. That's how I knew life was beating me with a stick. I sat at my desk in the second to last row in the room, in the back. I put my head down. Mr. Fracassi was teaching a Shakespeare play, and all of a sudden, I wasn't there.

"Pia, give your sister some of those turkey feathers," Dad gently urged. "You have four and she doesn't have any."

"Dad, I promise I will find her some of her own."

"You don't know that for sure," he answered back. We were inching closer to home.

"Yes, I do. I know" I told Dad sure of myself.

In about one minute, there were two nice-sized turkey feathers on the ground in front of me. My face lit up, and I yelled excitedly, "Dad! More feathers!" Delilah smiled from ear to ear. I handed them to her.

"Pia," Dad called. I didn't answer. I couldn't reach him. I felt him calling me again.

"Pia. Hurry up. We are almost home."

The entire class was staring at me. Mr. Fracassi was waiting for my reply. "You need to pay more attention, Pia," he said. The floodgates opened at that. "I'm sorry. I have to go" as I ugly cried out the door. I sat in the guidance office lobby for over an hour until they told me I should probably just sign myself out since I was eighteen. I left, and I wouldn't return to school for several days.

Since I had a sad birthday, I always tried so hard to make sure my loved ones felt special on theirs. I smiled for Tim even though it brought on a deep, sharp pain in my chest. Earl and I sat at the dining room table and sang him happy birthday. The late March sky was a December gray. I reminisced back to the day Tim was born. I could picture every inch of the hospital room, and the look on Mom's face when Dad brought Delilah and me in to meet our little brother. Earl was cutting the cake when my phone rang. I picked it up. It was my middle school drama teacher, the wife of my current drama teacher, who was good friends with the Finnley family.

She said, "Pia, are you sitting down?" The next thing I knew I was grabbing my keys and telling Earl, "I have to go. I have to go to Rose's house." He looked at me and said, "Pia" kind of loudly. I turned. He asked, "Are you okay to drive?" I shook my head, pretty sure of the fact that I could handle anything at this point. As I drove the back way from Ralley to Cherish, my brain shut off. I had no thoughts in my head. I just stared at the double yellow lines on the pavement as it got darker with each turn I made. I stood in Rose's house by the front door. Her parents had arrived home from church where they had led the choir in singing Rose into Heaven. They didn't know that's what they were doing at the time. Rose's last words were, "I see blue skies." My mind raced back to the day in the cul de sac when she smiled and told me her name. I could vividly picture her bangs and freckles. She met my mom. We swung on my rusted blue swing set toward the open blue sky.

Mr. Fracassi came to Rose's viewing. I walked up to him and said hello. He asked me to point out Rose's parents in the crowd. I pointed, literally, to them in the corner. He told me, "Do not point, Pia. It is considered rude. Thank you for showing me. I will make sure to say my condolences to them." Everyone stood in a circle and said the rosary. I stood by him the whole time. He said every word. Mr. Fracassi was Catholic. I knew that because he told me that he was named after a saint his parents held dear to their hearts. As I stood by him watching him recite the rosary with his student and his other student's family, I thought about how there was no other teacher like him. I found Gram and asked her to go find a straw so I could cut it in half. She was confused. I told her it was either that or cigarettes. Even though I was old enough to buy them as of December 24, 2014, I was still too scared to. Gram said, "I'll be right back." Minutes later, she handed me a pack of cigarettes, and I put them in my best friend's casket as a symbol from her favorite book and a nod to our costume duo.

Tomorrow was her funeral. I was dreading it. At one point, after most people had left, Mr. Finnley came up to me and said, "I'm sorry you have to go through this again. It's been too many times for you, kid." I wasn't sure he knew this at the time, but I wouldn't trade the years of knowing and loving Rose Finnley for all the pain to be removed in an instant. I know he felt the same way. Mrs. Finnley then found me and said, "Pia, we want you to know that you are more than welcome to ride with us tomorrow to the funeral and burial." I smiled lightly and told her I would like that. She told me where to be and what time to get there. A member of Relentless Glory Catholic Church had rented a limousine for the Finnleys for tomorrow so the whole family could ride as one. In the limousine would be Mr. and Mrs. Finnley, Josh and his girlfriend Emily, Jedediah, Jimmy, Rayne, Jamie, and me. I sat in the middle of the limo across from the bar. I had never been in a car with a bar. I had the sudden realization that Rose and I would never celebrate our 21st birthdays together.

We arrived at the banquet hall where Rose's funeral would

be held. It was owned by Relentless Glory and was being held there because the church was too small for this service. Many were expected. There was a spot in the front adjacent to the door designated for the Finnley's limousine to park. We walked inside. The walls by the front door were lined with people. On the left side a little further down, I saw my family. Aunt Jemma stood there in a black dress with Delilah by her side. Delilah had curled her hair; tears were forming in her eyes. She mouthed, "Love you."

Earl was dressed in a light brown suit, and Tim was next to him in a button-down dress shirt and bow tie. Aunt Natalie and Uncle Colt stood next to Tim. Alex and Jackson stood behind them. Next to Aunt Natalie and Uncle Colt was Gram. My red-haired cousin Ruby from my dad's side was there. I loved Ruby and was so glad to see her face. As I walked with the Finnleys, I waved to them. I made my way over and said quickly, "Thank you guys for coming. I'm going to take a look at the pulpit where I have to…y'know…speak in a little." They nodded, and I kept walking.

I walked through an open doorway to find more chairs crammed together than I had ever seen in my life. The chairs in the first two rows had names and yellow ribbons on them. I found my name and seat. I attached my ribbon to my dress. I first looked toward the stage. My eyes were met by many large flower bouquets. I then made sure to find the pulpit. I stood there taking in every square inch of the hall. I couldn't believe this was real. I pinched myself just to make sure. *Damn.* It was.

I was sorrowful but trying not to show it until after I spoke. I had to get through this for Rose. No one, not even myself, was going to stop me. When everyone was seated, or standing against the wall, I proceeded in with the Finnley family behind Rose's casket. I glanced over at my family briefly. I couldn't look long, or I'd lose my composure.

The time had come. I got up, my hands shaking as my pink high heels clutched the floor. I adjusted the mic and said, "The last time I did this was for my mom. Please give me a moment to get ready." I could hear people shudder. I began.

My name is Pia Haughman, Rose's best friend and unbiological sister. To you all, I am Pia, but to Rose, I am better known as her smoking-hot male costume partner. If you're wondering why I'm standing up here today, it's because Rose asked me to, and I told her yes.

I've known Rose for a long time. We grew up as next-door neighbors. As our friendship developed, we realized we were always there for one another and spent most of our time together.

I then recounted 3-4 solid, funny memories. Many of these fill the pages you now hold in your hands. I looked out into the crowd at Josh Finnley as I told the bike-hijacking story. He laughed. I continued.

You may be asking yourself, whether it be now or later, how I'm able to stand up here without getting emotional. Much like our friendship, that is not for you to understand. When a friend like Rose Finnley asks you to do something, it becomes less about how you'll make it through and more about finding a way to make it happen, for her.

Rose Finnley was a friend for every stage of life. She was the kind of friend you meet up with at a coffee shop when you're stressed out about your master's program. She was the kind of friend you send Christmas cards to with your children's pictures on them. She was the kind of friend who knew my greatest fear to my deepest hope.

You're probably also wondering how I'm able to stand up here with this being the first time I'm mentioning the word cancer. That's because that ugly word did not define her, and it never will. It doesn't deserve a place in the final say. I could tell you that I wish we had one more time, for the lake, to meet up at your house or mine, or to laugh until our stomachs ached.

That is selfish because you are in a much better place. I want you to know that I know many people are lined up to become honorary big sisters to your siblings. I want you to know that I am the first in line. And, if you don't mind me asking for just one final request... I ask that while I give your parents a hug for you today... you will do the same with mine.

I had to leave Rose's reception early. I couldn't dance. I couldn't socialize. All I wanted to do was lie in my bed and cry. That's exactly what I did, but first, I called my cousin Ruby. Ruby was a few years older than me, but she always knew what to say. She had two children who I believed had a mom who was truly meant to be a mother. I sent her a message and said, "Can I call?" She told me, "Of course you can. You did such a lovely job today, my beautiful little cousin. You amaze me, Pia."

We talked and then I lay in bed crying. Three days shy of two months later, I graduated high school with Raven by my side. Aunt Nellie, Uncle Frank, Juliana, Genevieve, and

Nico came down from Massachusetts for my graduation party at the Ralley house. I did everything I could to put on a smile for those who had shown up for me. A few days after my party, Aunt Nat and I took Aunt Nellie and her family into downtown Cherish to enjoy a nice day in the heart of town. Tim, Jackson, and Alex joined us too. After everyone had placed their order at my favorite coffee shop in town, Aunt Nellie sat down to wait for her drink. She picked up the local newspaper sitting on the wooden coffee table, smiled, and handed it to me. It featured a picture of me in my cap and gown holding a pink heart balloon and read, "18-year-old East High graduate Pia Haughman sends off a balloon to her best friend Rose Finnley the night of graduation." That was the second time in two months I had made the front cover of the newspaper. The first time was for a picture of my graduation cap that read, "Mom, Dad, and Rose, I did it!" I set the paper down and winked at Aunt Nellie.

"Looks like I'm famous," I joked.

Chapter 16
Darkness. Then Light.

I attempted to go off to college in North Carolina right after graduation. Everyone around me was doing it, and I thought I could handle it. I knew I wanted to receive a college education, and I was ready to get out of Virginia. The school was a little over four hours from Cherish, VA. When I got there, I knew in my soul it wasn't the right time for me to go off to school. I tried to pretend it was, and maybe it would be. Maybe if I pretended, it could be. I remember watching all the girls around me make friends and laugh, but all I could do was cry. I lost five pounds. Gram and Aunt Natalie drove back down on August 21, 2015, to get me. I left college eight short days after move-in day. When we arrived back in Cherish, we pulled into a pharmacy parking lot where Earl, Uncle Colt, and Tim Jr. got out to help unload my dorm room belongings into the bed of Earl's truck. I would move back in with Earl at the Ralley house again. It was time to go home until things were better, until I was better. Some people thought I didn't give it long enough, but I will always advocate for each person to do what is best for them when it comes to the major decisions in life. College is an expensive decision, and it should be done with careful thought. If a person isn't ready, they should wait. To add, when something isn't right, you know. I was incredibly self-aware for an 18-year-old.

    I enrolled at the local community college the next week. I also signed up to teach Sunday school at Relentless Glory, where I would be the fourth-grade assistant teacher. I had worked at a fancy restaurant in downtown Cherish before going off to school as a bus girl. I found another restaurant in town upon returning home where I would be a waitress, but I was given tables on my own way too soon and panicked. I told them I couldn't do it, and they said I was fine, waitressing wasn't for everyone. I went to work at a daycare instead. I also found a babysitting job two days a week for a professor at my community college. She taught math and had the cutest three-month-old baby.

In some ways, working with the kids was a lot harder than waitressing, but I enjoyed it so much more. I felt called to work with kids and often reflected on high school a few short months ago in Mr. Fracassi's class. When I was in my dorm room in North Carolina, I was, on paper, a psychology major. I felt I "had" to do something to help people based on the life I'd lived. I felt the obvious choice was to be a grief counselor. The more I thought about it, though, I didn't want to do that. That sounded terrible, but I wasn't sure of any other way to help kids who had gone through similar pain. I had dreaded my advanced placement psychology class in high school. The information was no doubt valuable, and it should have been interesting to me after all I had been through, but it just wasn't. I loved to write. I loved to play around with words, stringing them along to craft beautiful images in a person's mind. I loved to read Poe, Fitzgerald, Hemingway, and poetry by Emily Dickinson. I loved so many authors and poets. *How can I help people?* I thought. I heard a lightbulb in my head explode when I considered, *Didn't Mr. Fracassi help you?* Yes, I told myself. *So, could you become an English teacher like him: passionate, quirky, fun? A teacher who believes in your students? A teacher who lights a fire and that light is nearly impossible to burn out?* It hit me. I needed to be an English major. I knew what I wanted. I believe it was always in my destiny to write and teach English, even if I take breaks or do not do those things for my entire life.

The first semester at community college consisted of me taking remedial math classes worth one credit, if that, due to how poorly I did on my placement tests. There were a lot of days I wanted to throw in the towel. I made it through those, though. The spring of 2016 was when my first real semester of college happened. I hadn't had the confidence to take an AP test in high school, but I had done all the work of the advanced placement classes. Therefore, I sat in a 100-level English class I felt I was way ahead of, but I had to complete it in order to move forward. I also had a history class called Western Civilization on my schedule. One night around 8:00, I texted Uncle Colt, "Can I come over? I have a history paper on 'What makes a great leader?' and I'm stumped."

For some reason, writing a history paper was more difficult than writing a literary analysis, and I hadn't quite mastered that skill yet. Uncle Colt loved history almost as much as he loved soccer and was a skilled writer, so I knew he'd be able to help. He responded a minute later, "Yep. You are always welcome over." When I got there, we visited like usual. Aunt Natalie sat on the couch next to Uncle Colt, and we talked about life, religion, how weird it was, in my opinion, to be nineteen, and the hockey team we liked...we pretty much talked about everything. We usually did this when I came over to visit because I could truly talk to them about all of life. Aunt Natalie eventually went to bed, and the boys were downstairs playing video games. Uncle Colt sat at the table with me where he had helped me through so many math problems and high school essays. He broke down the prompt for my history paper. We discussed qualities I thought made a good leader, and he gave his opinion. He even called his friend Alan and said, "Got a question for you!" Alan said he'd have to call Colt back. He was at a sports banquet with his kids.

Uncle Colt was going to ask Alan for his opinion on the great leader topic. Once my paper was well underway, I said, "Thank you so much for helping me, Uncle Colt. I should head home. I have to teach Sunday school pretty early in the morning." He said, "You sure you don't want to spend the night?"

"I would if I had my church clothes! Thank you though!" He said alright, told me to be careful and have a good night, and I walked out the door with my computer.

I got home at almost midnight. I played on my phone for about ten minutes and then crashed. I did have to be up early. In the middle of the night, I heard Earl's cell phone ring. He was hardcore "out of it," so it took him a second to realize what whoever called him was saying. The next thing I knew, my bedroom door was being swung open. Earl started shaking me, yelling, "Pia! *Pia?*" He was shaking me hard. I was asleep, but the kind of asleep where you can hear what's going on around you. We can call it a light sleep. I remember saying, "What the hell is wrong with you? Get off me! I'm fine! I'm right here! I'm *asleep.*"

The next morning, I could hear Gram in the kitchen talking to Earl. My brain went spiraling for a second. The feeling came back. Gram wasn't supposed to be here, paired with the way Earl stormed into my room last night to check on me. Someone died, and I just knew it. I walked into the kitchen skeptically, and slowly. Gram looked at me. I started to make coffee. "What are you doing here?" I asked her. As I inched closer to the table in the kitchen, she said, "Pia, I have to tell you something. Will you please sit down?" I scrunched my face up as I sat down at the kitchen table next to her. She said, "Uncle Colt died last night."

"What?" I exclaimed. She nodded. I said, "Is this a joke? It's not a funny one." She continued, "It is not a joke, Pia."

"Well, I was just with him last night, so I don't see how that's possible." She just stared into my soul. I said, "What happened? He just helped me write a history paper, literally not even twelve hours ago. It's fresh on the computer. I may not have even closed the document." I stood up. She asked me to sit back down.

Uncle Colt died of a gunshot wound in his home, my former home, a few minutes after I left. It was truly horrific for all who were there that night, especially for his oldest son Alex. Since I hadn't spent the night as Uncle Colt had offered for me to, I was not one of those people. I was, however, the last person to ever speak to Uncle Colt on Earth.

This sent me into the darkest place I had ever been in my life. It was early February of 2016. It was less than a year after Rose had died. I didn't know what to do. I dropped all my classes at community college except for one, which I failed. I had no parents, no Rose, no Uncle Colt, and I slipped into the deepest lie that I had no future. I didn't see my life working out in any positive way. How could it? I was a college dropout, a failure. I was so far in grief that I felt there was no way out.

Darkness had overcome me. It was all around. There were so many details and so many things to say about this time in my life, but I was nineteen, and I was hopeless. I went into a gas station to get an energy drink on February 7, 2016, the morning after finding out. My eyes were so swollen, I'm pretty sure the cashier thought I was high, even though I had never touched weed or any substance in my entire life, nor would I ever. I painted my car the day of Uncle Colt's funeral. It was painted with our inside jokes. No one got them, but his best friend from high school came up to me in the parking lot and said he appreciated that I did that for him. We agreed he was one hell of a person.

I spoke again at Uncle Colt's funeral. I started with a joke like he would have expected. I spoke about how he took us in and did the best he could for us. I told his friends and family how he created the sun to keep us company during our endless December. I told the audience what kind of Uncle Colt MacPherson was and how much happiness he brought to all of our lives. I did the best I could for him that day. Uncle Colt's friend Alan, who he had called as we worked on my paper, friended and reached out to me on social media. He was heartbroken. By the time he went to call my uncle back after the banquet ended, Uncle Colt was already gone. He said he knew how much I meant to Colt because Colt had told him, and that he was there for me. He signed off "a friend through Colt." His name sounded familiar, and he looked familiar too. I figured out later it was because they used to live in Uncle Colt and Aunt Natalie's neighborhood, and we had gone to the pool with Alan and his kids when Mom was here. I had forgotten about the days Mom had taken us to the pool with Aunt Natalie. My heart broke most for Aunt Natalie,

Alex, and Jackson. They had taken us in after we lost our parents. Alex and Jackson weren't supposed to lose a parent as teenagers. It didn't seem right. I had to be interviewed by the police since I was the last person to see my uncle alive. I told them he was his usual, regular self. I hadn't noticed *any* odd behavior. We talked; we wrote a kickass paper. Then, I left and woke up to a nightmare.

I remember one day, I went over to the Finnleys after Uncle Colt's passing. I was having such a hard time, and I just needed to be in the presence of people who understood. I told the Finnleys that my faith was terrible. I forget the context, but it was something I was feeling as I was surrounded by deep grief. I will never forget it. Mr. Finnley turned to me and said, "Girl, your faith is like gold tested in fire." From that point on, my perspective was different on my faith. I went a little easier on myself because I knew he was right.

March of 2016 arrived. I sat in the Ralley house surrounded by Mom's things, her absence and the emptiness of the home made me shiver. I was drowning in an ocean of deep pain. I knew how much I had around me in Earl, Tim, and so many others, but I had never quite been able to beat my depression before, and now it seemed impossible. I wanted to take my life, and I thought about how to do it. I always thought about Delilah and Tim after those thoughts traced my mind. They would be the only reason I would stay. I tried so hard to want to stay for them, but the suicidal thoughts and ideations would not cease. I thought about people sharing my obituary from my hometown and saying something like, "How sad. She couldn't even make it one year without her best friend." Everywhere I looked, no one understood the dark valley I was in. Social media was full of my classmates from high school living it up in college, smiling with new friends. Here I was, grieving my best friend times two. I didn't tell many people about how I was struggling at the time. I am not 100% sure why I didn't. It's possible I didn't want to burden others with my pain. It's possible that I also thought I wouldn't be taken seriously, and that's not me saying anything negative about anyone in my life. People always thought I was the strong girl who carried it all. I questioned if I would be understood at that moment. It would've been met with "Oh, but you're so strong!" I want people to understand that the people you think are the strongest are the ones you need to check on. The people who laugh and smile can be the ones battling suicidal thoughts.

It was now early June of 2016, and I was on a trip to Florida. While I was there, toward the end of the trip, I visited the house of a favorite writer of mine. He is remembered by the name of Mr. Ernest Hemingway. The house was massive and intricate. Cats were walking around, some with six toes because they were descendants of the real cats Hemingway had when he was alive. The house was white, two stories, had numerous bright green shutters and was surrounded by waving palm trees. Inside were his old typewriters, books, belongings, and close to one hundred people. As I watched all these people walking around Hemingway's house years after he had been gone, snapping photos, it did something to me. I was saved that day in Florida. I believe I have been saved a few times in my life: that day at the lake when my dad jumped in fully clothed to save me from drowning and this day at Hemingway's house in Florida. I was slapped in the face by the reality that my life had a purpose and needed to be lived. I couldn't allow the darkness to take over. People needed to hear my story. The tour guide showed me the room Hemingway wrote in from 6 am to 12 pm each day. I committed myself to the rest of my life standing in Hemingway's writing oasis. Whatever was to come, I would be there.

Hemingway suffered in many of the same ways I did but for different reasons. I can't say he would've loved my writing, but the legacy I saw live on in his house that day due to the courage he had to write and share his writing with the world is a big reason I can write this today.

I took a long time to graduate from community college because I was only a part-time student my entire time there, but I was committed to everything in my life, even this. I called my friend Brady from the hockey internet world and told him one day that I thought I would never finish college. I was still working on the whole being positive thing. He always said he knew I would. He encouraged me to keep going because I was going to be a great teacher, but he also reminded me there was nothing wrong with taking a semester off if needed. I needed another break, so I listened to Brady. I remember babysitting at nineteen and twenty years old for families in their thirties with gorgeous homes, wondering if I would ever be done with this stage of my life, wondering if I would ever have that. I did not come up with the idea that comparison is the thief of joy. I agree comparison is a thief, but I think it is a thief of perspective. Every time I compared my situation to someone else's, I lost sight of how beautifully I was doing after so much darkness. I lost my perspective in comparing.

I graduated with my associate's degree on May 14, 2019.

In August of 2019, I transferred to a university as an English major planning to apply to the education program that semester. The school was a small, private university only an hour and five minutes from Cherish. I had one normal semester at my college, but I received the confirmation in that first and only normal semester that I was exactly where I was supposed to be doing exactly what God had made me to do. The world and my school were shut down shortly after due to a global pandemic. My university time was a whirlwind, much like my childhood. I was a little disappointed because I anticipated transferring to a university and being able to delve into literature with a certain peace of mind after spending so long at community college and struggling so much. I didn't get that due to the chaos the pandemic caused in the world and the world of education.

My success in college was only made possible due to the most amazing stepfather, Earl, and grandmother, Gram. I lived with Earl all of community college, but on and off with both Gram and Earl during my university years. Earl got up each day and went to work past his retirement age, lifting heavy boxes in a warehouse with no air-conditioning so that Tim and I could have health insurance and a place to live as Tim finished high school and I finished college. He is truly the most selfless, wonderful person I know still to this day. Gram let me drive her car to school a few days a week when I commuted my first year of university, so my car didn't have to take on all of that mileage. She made me coffee and gave me pep talks. She made me believe I could do it. Raven and I spent many of my college years going for margaritas every once in a while and hanging out on the regular. Penny would remind me I am "blessed and highly favored."

I started to believe it. I had grown close to Rose's siblings Rayne and Jedediah in particular, and Aria, Rose's friend from science class, had become one of my good friends.

At the end of my first semester of university life, Brady and I began dating. He had always cared about me, and that was a gift. I knew I had someone who not only cared about me but whom I greatly trusted. He didn't judge me for the life I'd had. Delilah and I had become a lot closer, and well, Tim was Tim. Alan and his family became the biggest blessing from such a horrible situation. Ernest Hemingway once said, "The world breaks everyone, and afterward, some are strong at the broken places." I hope he would consider me one of the "some."

This is one chapter of my story I wish had been different. Uncle Colt was one of the best men I will ever know. He is a huge part of my perseverance. As I was reflecting on this time of darkness in my life, I reflected on how easy it was to fall into hopelessness when down in the valley of life. It's so easy in the valley to fall into the lie that life will never get better, that the terrible time you are currently in will be the case for the rest of your life. I want everyone reading this to know how dangerous and evil that lie is. I don't know where you are as you hold this book in your hands. I don't know what difficulties you find yourself facing. Perhaps they feel insurmountable to you at this very moment. I want you to know you will find the light again. You will make it through to the other side. You cannot judge your life while the disaster is going on. It is when the storm is over that the clouds part, the sun comes out, and rays of light hit our faces. It's then we can see what has bloomed. It's hard to see the beauty that has bloomed when it is dark, and debris is flying everywhere.

Do not make a judgment about your life until you are in the right frame of mind to do so, until you have held those beautiful blooms in your hand and breathed in the air around them. Life will always come with struggle; we live in a broken world. That isn't going away. Even when life is wonderful, it will never be perfect. There are so many ways my life doesn't look like I thought it would. Just like all beautiful things and people do not look the same, such is true for life. Do not compare. Social media doesn't tell all. As you talk to people, and I mean *really* talk to them, you find that you are not so uncommon. You are not so far away from others. I will always have to tread through life with care because I feel deeply; therefore, situations affect me more.

I have overcome a lot, and in many ways, I am stronger than I should be. The flip side of that is a little more unseen. I struggle more each time I face grief due to experiencing so much of it so young. Grief isn't just death; there are many situations we encounter in life that force us to grieve. I have to feel slowly because I feel intensely. I have to take challenges one piece at a time because earlier this year I was confronted with the unpleasant truth that living in survival mode for so long has taken a toll on my physical health. People don't usually talk about the physical toll having to be constantly strong takes on a person, so I had no idea it would slap me in the face. I have to understand that life will always be simultaneously devastating and exhilarating, a portion of a quote I got from the real Earl Rhoades.

Watching Earl get up each day and be a father to us three kids when he owed us absolutely nothing helped me on many occasions tap into my strength. I never thought I would feel called to write an almost 60,000-word memoir at twenty-seven years of age. I really do feel that at twenty-seven, I have fully experienced many facets of life most don't until they are much, much older. In many ways, it's a blessing to have already lived a full life. For every heartbreaking experience, God has given me 20 more wonderful ones, not to mention the phenomenal human beings he has placed in my life to help me. Despite being a deeply feeling person in a broken world, despite the deep heartbreak I've experienced too young, my life is still beautiful. When I sit with that, it's amazing, and there's so much more to come, exhilarating and devastating. I think that's why they call life a mystery.

Chapter 17

Reflection on Deep Loss

When I think about the most difficult parts of losing my parents by age 14, I am confronted with all of the moments I didn't have them for since then. Some of those moments are big things like my high school and college graduations or my wedding, and it makes me so sad to think about never getting to experience my parents as grandparents when I do have children. I'll never get to call my mom for parenting advice or see my dad push my daughter in a wheelbarrow. They would've been the best of the best. Most of the moments I struggle in though are little moments in the everyday. Those little moments are where I've felt a hard reminder of what I've lost. My mom used to tell me long before she knew she was sick and would die, "No one loves you like your parents." If you are blessed with good ones like me, it rings true. In my younger 20s, I wrote a Facebook post about missing my mom and wanting to ask her a few things. I then wrote, "I guess the most self-assuring thing is that I've learned to become everything I need." I want to mention this because I do believe it. When you lose your parents young, you do not lose your relationship with them for the rest of your life. That relationship just looks different. I have listened close to my heart--the very heart that formed inside of my mom's body 27 years ago--to hear what my mom or dad would say. I have looked for signs and found them in numbers, passing the same make and model truck my dad used to have, flowers, butterflies, people's stories, and much more. I've prayed for them to show me the way. I have reflected on experiences we shared where I went through something similar and remembered what they said. I have read their cards, letters, and my baby book. I have stared at so many old photographs and found my way in their loving smiles frozen in time as long as the photographs remain. I have confided in my siblings who will always be my little part of them on Earth.

On another note, I tend to feel a little bad when I reflect on life without my parents because in a way it feels as if I'm forgetting about the wonderful people who have stepped up for me. I have to remind myself just like I wrote earlier in this book that two things can be true at once. I am always going to miss my parents' physical presence in this life; however, I am always going to be grateful for the people God has sent me. My grandmother is a wonderful woman. I have called her many, MANY times when needing advice or to talk. She has listened and helped me through so much. In a way, it's sweet hearing from the woman who helped my mom when she was a young woman needing advice too. It is such a blessing to have her. I will never take our years together for granted. My stepfather is a wonderful man. I got to experience a father's love twice in this life. Words cannot express how much he means to me or how much our relationship has bettered my life, forever. On my wedding day, I wrote both my grandmother and stepfather a letter letting them know how much I love them and all they've meant to me throughout my life. It was detailed. I will leave that letter between us, but it captured everything in my heart I ever wanted to say. I think everyone should do that for loved ones on their wedding day who have played a huge role. It was difficult to write, as was this book, but so worth it. I spent the weeks leading up to my wedding crying as I wrote these letters, and I questioned myself because who wants to spend the weeks before their wedding in tears? I am so glad I did this! I challenge everyone reading this to write the hard things. It doesn't have to be your wedding day to do so. I just know I will always be grateful I let my grandmother and stepfather know what had been sitting in the deepest parts of my heart. I can't say I came up with that idea myself. It was an idea of my Uncle Colt's. He told me when I was living with him that he did the same thing for his parents on his wedding day. My life is particularly beautiful because the tragedies I've endured have put me directly on the path to becoming acquainted with others who I may have not known or not known as well. There is no way to know what my life would have looked like had things been different, but it would likely look like a different life. The mothers of my friends have stepped up in my life to help me, and I am eternally grateful for Mrs. Finnley and Penny who both knew and loved my mom. I have grown close to my Aunt Natalie and have confided in her and asked her questions about my mom. I have numerous aunts and uncles on my father's side that I can confide in. To add, I know when the time comes, my children will have so many "adopted grandmothers" and one beautiful guardian angel on my side.

 Life without the beautiful Rose Finnley is something I'll struggle with until my last day. I have so many wonderful friends, but nothing will ever completely take away the sting of Rose's absence. I am blessed with friends who knew and loved Rose too. Rose's sister in particular has been the greatest blessing. I know Rose smiles so much seeing Rayne and I's bond. All of Rose's siblings and her entire family have blessed me in ways I can't even count. When I think back to Rose's funeral as I stood up there reading her eulogy, I knew way back then it was going to be difficult. I had already lost my parents, so it hasn't been a surprise to me how painful life without my best friend has been. I still don't think I was fully prepared. As I sit on my bed writing this, Rose's 28th birthday will be later this year. 10 years will soon have passed since I celebrated a birthday with my best friend. A few months after that will mark 10 years since I last saw her. It gets easier each year, but it also doesn't. Grief is not only the longest journey but also a great contradiction. How can it get easier but remain just as difficult? When it comes to grief, I've realized I'll never understand her. I've spent a lot of time with grief over the years, and I have to tell you. I don't think grief wants to be understood. She simply stands in the spot of my friend to remind me that I once loved someone who is no longer here and that I still love her. Grief is honestly a damn loyal friend. She never leaves me…even though I wish she would. Yet, to wish she would leave would mean a part of what I've lost leaves forever, too. So, I ask her to stay. Sometimes I make her stand rooms away from me; other times she sits next to me on the couch. Other times, she slaps me across the face. This is usually on birthdays and holidays. You might be wondering…yes…just because I said Grief was a loyal friend doesn't mean she's a nice one. She's kind of terrible, but it's not her fault. She's just doing her job. I've visited Rose probably over 40 times and watched her cemetery fill up. Each time I visit her, I not only reflect on that but also on how much I've watched myself change as I've sat in front of her headstone the last decade. Each time, I feel strongly that there is a piece inside of me that will always be the Pia Haughman who Rose met in the cul-de-sac on that sunny day. I think there's something beautiful about that.

    The loss of my Uncle Colt will always stand as the most tragic thing I've ever known. It was the fourth major loss in my life, and it almost ended everything for me. Suicide is never the answer, and I say grief from suicide is its own kind of heartbreakingly terrible. The best course of action if you are struggling is to confide in those you love and trust, and then to seek help. It is okay if you have to seek help multiple times. Healing is not linear. It's not a one-and-done. Keep fighting because you deserve to see the beauty of your future. You deserve to see all the roles you will grow into and all the people who will love you. The way Uncle Colt died was so devastating paired with how unexpected it was and the fact that I had just been there. I questioned myself for not spending the night that night like he had offered. I questioned myself for even going over that night. I could've written that paper by myself. It was truly the most horrific experience. The night of Colt MacPherson's death will never make sense to me. He was the happiest person I knew. He was a loving husband, father, son, uncle, and friend. It's been hard for me to understand why and how it happened the night I had just been there and in that way. I've come to understand that I was constantly told by everyone around me that I was the strongest person they knew, and I still became enveloped by darkness. The happiest, strongest person in your life can be struggling. Check on your happy friends and family. Check on the strongest person you know. Take time to be with yourself to understand how you are really doing and know that it is okay to be doing poorly. If you find you are doing poorly, seek guidance and help.

Due to my life story, I have been given the gift of knowing people in a different or greater capacity. Because of this, I get to love more. I know this also means I will grieve more. I don't look forward to losing the people who I know and love in a greater way, but I understand that grief is simply the after-effect of love. Even though I will never understand why I had to be the recipient of many extremely unfortunate events, my human mind finds comfort in the good people and things that have come out of the tragedies. I am not sure I would have felt called to write a book about my life in my twenties had I not lost my parents at age 14 and my best friend just four years later. I have made peace with the fact that I will never know why and have found things to be grateful for despite the life I've endured. I don't know anyone with a stepfather like mine. I know very few people who have a male role model in their life who is even a quarter like Earl. I know no one with a sibling bond like mine. I have always wanted to use my pain for good. It would have been a lot easier to continue a life of pain. It takes work to choose perseverance to the other side. It takes work to find the light and walk in it. The work I speak of usually leads us to the brightest and happiest moments of our lives. I want to make it clear that the work I speak of is daily work. Every day I have to battle the negative thoughts and comfort the heart of the little girl who rode her bike down Linsell Lane. You don't wake up one day and have this large realization of, "I'm healed." Each day I wake up, I still love my parents. This means, I still grieve. You can grieve and celebrate, grieve and smile. That is what I have always tried to do. It is well worth the work.

Some of the very best moments of my later childhood

as I have reflected were the years where, while I was in them, I didn't appreciate enough. They were the moments with Rose, life in the MacHaughman household, visiting Gram regularly, and living with Earl at the Ralley house. During these years, my life was hard, and maybe that's why I failed to truly understand their value. If you are ever looking ahead or wishing things were different, I want you to stop and think to yourself, "These are the good days." Even if that feels crazy at the time, really reflect on that, and soak the present in. What can you appreciate right now? There's always something. Perhaps the very best moments of our lives are the moments where we are in the thick of it but look around at the beautiful people around us. We are often met with the gaze of people who have stepped in and stepped up for us. These people could have chosen to be doing anything else; they could have easily turned the other cheek and had an easier time. The people who truly love us will be there. They may not be able to fix everything, but they will be present to guide and give what they can. The true test of love isn't fixing everything for someone or even giving someone everything, it is simply being there in the dark with that person, when you don't have to be. It's showing up in little ways that when you look back, mean everything.

Chapter 18

Amidst the Peonies

The time came to sell the Ralley house. About six months before the house was to sell, I hired a local photographer to come out to our house. Gram brought Delilah over. The photographer took pictures of us in the yard, on Mom's precious white couches that had been with us since our Linsell days, sitting in Earl's truck, and out back overlooking the Ralley backyard. She also took pictures of Earl and Gram holding Mom's picture. She was with us and in everything we did. After the photographer left, Delilah said to me, "You know, Pia. I always felt you and Tim were stronger than me for staying in Cherish and moving back to this house. Now that we're selling it, I wish I could take it all back. I wish I could have looked at this place more positively during the pain. We were so lucky to have a place that gave us a tangible reminder of Mom's presence." I put my arm around her as we walked toward the gravel road.

Tim graduated the following month. I always felt bad when I thought about Tim's senior year being taken over by a pandemic. I always thought he deserved so much more out of life. He was so young when we lost our parents. When I talked to Tim about this, he told me he got to miss two months of school, so he was okay with it. Yes, that was true, and it was the typical teenage boy response that was supposed to make you laugh. I was accepted into the teaching program at my university. I completed all my classroom hours and then student-taught during the pandemic. This time was grueling mentally and academically. It was no walk in the park. During the pandemic, Penny became sick and was placed in a medically induced coma. I stayed with Raven during my student-teaching two to three days a week, so she didn't have to be alone during her mom's illness. I knew how difficult having a sick mom was. I cherished being able to support her during those times, and Penny made it through her illness. The odds were less than one percent.

I fell in love with my friend Brady while the world was falling apart, and we drove down the west side of the state every two weeks to see each other while I completed my bachelor's degree. I graduated with my bachelor's degree in English with an undergraduate certificate and teaching certification on May 23, 2021, magna cum laude. Yes, you can graduate magna cum laude even if you had to take a break, even if you failed, and even if you have been through more turmoil than you can count.

Aunt Natalie watched the recording of my graduation online while Earl, Gram, Tim, and Brady joined me in person. Following graduation, I moved three hours from Cherish to a different part of my home state to be closer to Brady where I accepted my first teaching position. It was time, but it was still hard to move away from such a heartbreaking but special place. I reflected a lot on moving from Cherish. I had never understood how a place could make me so happy and so sad at the same time. It's much like the realization that life would be both exhilarating and devastating, a mystery. Cherish was where it all began. It felt like home in a life that had taken so much. For that reason, I would always love it. People could say whatever they wanted about Cherish, and they did. It would always be different for me. I didn't expect anyone to get that.

I began teaching at a rural school in a town where I knew no one. It was terrifying to be a first-year teacher in a brand-new place, but I already had confidence that I could do just about anything. Throwing in the pandemic that was still going on, it was a challenge to be a first-year teacher. As a teacher, I had a special place in my heart for the students going through difficulties, whatever that looked like. I connected with my students by showing passion for the content I taught. I hoped by showing up in the little ways, they would become empowered to know they could show up for themselves, too. Mr. Fracassi would always be such a big part of the teacher I was.

Brady asked me to marry him at the end of my first year of teaching. He asked me at a duck pond we had visited several times while doing long-distance, in front of just me. We have no picture of the moment; it lives in our minds for just the two of us. I had told him I didn't want the proposal to be a big thing due to my anxiety. I said yes. Our wedding took place fourteen months later, in August, at our church. As the car pulled up to the front of the beautiful church we would be married in, I looked up to see Earl. He walked out and opened the wooden church doors to get me. Next to him was Tim Jr. They both walked me down the aisle. Delilah was my maid of honor, and next to me were my wonderful friends. Many of the Haughmans were there, the Finnleys were there, and my Massachusetts family had made the trip down. Of course, Brady's family and friends, too. So many loved ones surrounded us. The biggest surprise of the day was Delilah's maid of honor speech. She wrote a detailed poem. Though it is in my memoir, I cannot take credit for it. It is all Delilah. It spoke of our painful childhood, our sibling bond, my favorite things in life, and our strength. The room was quiet, and the lights dimmed. As the background music played, Delilah said,

On 33 Linsell Lane, our childhood home, where memories bloom like wildflowers roam.

Through the toughest storms, we fought our way, uncertain if dawn would ever replace the gray. But now here we stand, stronger than ever, bound by a bond time can't sever.

Pia, my sister, my guiding light. You've lifted me through the darkest night.

Amidst the peonies, love's bloom will start, a tribute to Mom and Dad, forever in our hearts. As you build a life strong and true, know that their love lives on through you.

Afterward

Alfred Lord Tennyson once wrote:

"'Tis better to have loved and lost

Than never to have loved at all."

We have pondered this quote from his elegy for years. Many people hold their opinions on whether or not it is true. I hope to have answered the question. I consider us, those who have truly known honest love and felt the painful sting of loss, the lucky ones. To have never experienced my father's smile of hope, my mother's strength, my best friend's spirit, or my uncle's deep dedication would have stripped my life bare at its start. I believe that if Tennyson's quote was a lie, people wouldn't love again after heartbreak, in any capacity. What would be the point?

Yet almost everyone does go on to show love in this world after loss. Love gives life meaning, and we all need love. Our bodies and minds crave it. This is a broken world where we will lose the people we love, sometimes too soon. We are all temporary. Everything here is. This is a reason to love and appreciate every moment, not a reason to run from it or wish it had never been a part of our life at all. For a long time, I felt I was alone in the amount of loss and the depth of loss I had experienced. It branded me as an outsider from everyone in the world. The more I've spoken to people and the more I sat with my grief, the more I began to understand how many souls share an experience I've had and how many people my story could help. I was never alone, even when I felt it.

    I had to let my story sit with me. I had to sit alone with it and study it. We had some painful stare-downs because I had to get to know it before I could begin the long and arduous journey of writing about it. One day, I asked my academic advisor at community college why he thought I couldn't write this book…or anything for that matter. Why did he think I was so numb? Why did I call myself a writer but couldn't actually write? He looked at me and said, "Paige, it's one of those stories that needs to sit in your soul for 20 years before you can write about it." He was right.

    It was important for me to wait until I hit an age where I was mature enough to write from a place of both honesty and consideration. If I had written this in my earlier years, it would have been a story tainted with anger and hurt. The truth is, I started this story in six to eight notebooks throughout my life, beginning my junior year of high school through my college years. Yet, I would always stop three to four pages in. I began this adventure again in early October of 2023, a few months after getting married, to complete applications to graduate school for creative writing. The programs I applied to were extremely competitive, and I was rejected from every single one. I was trying to write this story from an entirely fictional standpoint, but this story was always meant to be a memoir with some creative touches. The rejections hurt, and I let them hurt me. This story was something so personal to me. I checked my email shortly after the rejections to find an email from a friend by the name of Dr. Kelly Huff who wrote, "If you want to write, just write, Paige. You have all you need." I knew she was right. Thank you, Dr. Huff, for the inspiration to go for it.

There have been so many excuses I've made not to do this: I didn't get into grad school, so my story must be terrible, people might judge me, it may never sell, and it will be painful to write. The list goes on. The truth is it takes so much within me to share this with the world. I know I will possibly face negative feedback for sharing my story. They will be the ones who leave negative reviews or make me question if writing this book was the right decision. I want to make something crystal clear: this book was not written for those people. This is something I feel called to do for the people who need it, and I would've held myself back from sharing this with the world if I hadn't forced myself to write it. The fear of being eighty or ninety years old, if God lets me see those years, and never having written my book shook me to my core. I couldn't bear the thought of it being too late and never having done it. I did not share every detail. I kept many things to myself and my family, but what I have shared is special and can bring so much to readers.

I've thought a lot about what the purpose of this book is. When I think about that, I keep thinking about all the kids in the world who have gone through losing both of their parents and didn't have an Earl, an Aunt Nat and Uncle Colt, a Rose Finnley, or an Alan. Some children lose their parents and don't have siblings to lean on or a grandmother who helps out. I believe this book is for them. God has put people in my life who have helped me. I am undeserving. My heart breaks for the kids who don't have that. I hope they find comfort in my story.

My first hope is that my story brings awareness to the

areas of our shared human experience that are rushed past but never fully known, areas like grief, healing, addiction struggles, mental health awareness, and trauma. I hope it helps to decrease the stigma around all of them. People who have experienced trauma as children can and do go on to lead successful, productive lives. They do not all choose to continue a life of darkness and pain, and we should never assume that a person who has experienced trauma cannot live a fulfilling life. My second hope is for my loved ones in my story who were stripped of time. May they impact others through my writing because I am certain they would have gone on to make a difference in the lives of so many had they not been taken so soon. Let it be them who inspire you and not me. I just wrote about knowing them. My third hope is for this book to embrace others who have experienced deep loss in their darkest hours. May it encourage them to make the brave decision to carry on. I want to leave you with this, and I hope it gives you something to consider. I still have many difficult days, and my family in my story still struggles in a variety of ways. Yet, though moments in life have been and can still be frigid, I find comfort in realizing I have known the best souls life has to offer. And that will always be enough to keep me company, each and every December.

About The Author

Paige Smith (Hockman) is a wife, writer, big sister, and a teacher at heart. She writes and speaks about the complexities of the human experience to help young people overcome their grief and challenges. She is a lover of coffee and the great American writers of the nineteenth and twentieth centuries. She holds a Bachelor of Arts in English from Shenandoah University, where she honed and explored her passion for literature and writing. She has taught 8th, 9th, and 10th grade English. Her life experience has shaped her understanding of young minds while inspiring her to explore themes of hardship, resilience, and personal growth in her writing. She lives in Virginia with her husband and their dog, Buddy, and cat, Boots. Her story tells the rest.

"December's Company" marks the beginning of Paige's literary career as her debut book. You can follow Paige on Instagram @perseveringpagebypaige to stay updated on her latest projects, writing, and literary endeavors.

Printed in the USA
CPSIA information can be obtained
at www.ICGtesting.com
CBHW051407081024
15567CB00036B/1009